Cinderella Didn't Live Happily Ever After

The Hidden Messages in Fairy Tales

Anne E. Beall, PhD

CINDERELLA DIDN'T LIVE HAPPILY EVER AFTER
The Hidden Messages in Fairy Tales

Cover Designed by Anne E. Beall

ISBN: 9781731285621

Also by Anne E. Beall

Reading the Hidden Communications Around You: A Guide to Reading the Body Language of Customers and Colleagues
https://www.amazon.com/s?k=beall+and+reading+the+hidden+communications&ref=nb_sb_noss

Strategic Market Research: A Guide to Conducting Research that Drives Businesses (3rd Edition)
https://www.amazon.com/Strategic-Market-Research-Conducting-Businesses/dp/173138517X/ref=sr_1_1?ie=UTF8&qid=1547756566&sr=8-1&keywords=strategic+market+research++anne+beall

Heartfelt Connections: How Animals and People Help One Another
https://www.amazon.com/s?k=Heartfelt+Connections+by+anne+beall&i=stripbooks&ref=nb_sb_noss

Community Cats: A Journey Into the World of Feral Cats
https://www.amazon.com/s?k=community+cats%3A+a+journey+by+anne+beall&ref=nb_sb_noss

The Psychology of Gender
https://www.amazon.com/Psychology-Gender-Second-Alice-Eagly/dp/1593852444/ref=sr_1_9?s=books&ie=UTF8&qid=1545485881&sr=1-9&keywords=psychology+of+gender

For Kristen and Owen Hensley, who have helped me immeasurably.

Contents

Tables

"Fairy tales do not tell children the dragons exist. Children already know that dragons exist. Fairy tales tell children the dragons can be killed."

—G.K. CHESTERTON

"If you want your children to be intelligent, read them fairy tales. If you want them to be more intelligent, read them more fairy tales."

—ALBERT EINSTEIN

Acknowledgements

I would like to thank many people who encouraged me to write this book and who believed it had a powerful message to convey. Several of the writers in my writing group (Friends with Words) encouraged me to finish this work and to get it out to as many people as possible.

I'd also like to thank my colleagues at Beall Research who listened to a presentation about the data and had many helpful comments. I'd specifically like to thank Helen Argiroff-Flood, who coded 129 of the Grimms' fairy tales.

Kristen Hensley, my dearest friend, often encouraged me to finish the book when the analyses and writing became arduous. She believed this work was important to share. I'll always appreciate her.

I also want to thank Jin A. Lee for her fabulous illustrations and ability to convey all kinds of feelings with the stroke of a pen. I communicated very little in my requests and she was able to express so much in her drawings. She's truly talented.

Another person I'd like to thank is Jill McKellan for her editing work. I appreciated her ability to take some of my clunky sentences and make them flow.

Lastly, I'd like to thank the many people whom I told about this book in casual conversations who said they couldn't wait to read it. You propelled me onward in this work with all your enthusiasm.

--Anne Beall, Chicago

Preface

On a recent visit to California to see friends, I was introduced to a large, masculine man. The kind of guy who would look great with an axe in his hand, chopping down a large tree. We had only talked for a few minutes when he revealed he would be getting married soon and was looking forward to his fairy tale wedding. I was struck by the word *fairy tale*; I hadn't expected *that* word from such a manly man. I asked him what he envisioned and he described a luxurious event where he, his bride, and his guests were treated like royalty. He also described how our mutual friend treats his wife like a *princess*.

While writing this book, I was struck by how often I have heard the words "fairy tale," "prince charming," "princess," "queen," and "king" in everyday conversation. Once you start listening for these words, you realize the prevalence of them. We use these words often; their underlying concepts are ones used to describe our lives and our dreams. And these ideas have a power of their own because they help us frame our lives. One of my friends has a saying in her home that she gave to her husband, which says: "You're my happily ever after." I believe all of us wish for some version of the fairy tale life where we find our version of the "handsome prince" or "beautiful princess."

Fairy tales hold a special place in our lives—we become familiar with them when we're young and they hold a magical power from that day forward. Perhaps we believe the stories we were told as children are actually true somewhere in the world and that impossible things can actually occur. And maybe royal people do live magical lives and occasionally marry common people. I believe that's why the royal weddings are such watched events and why royalty, who often have little power in countries, still exist. They represent an ideal.

Fairy tales also impart messages to us that things will work out for the best and we can overcome tremendous odds—just like the characters who seem to have everything against them but still triumph over those more powerful. These stories provide us with examples of children overcoming witches, average men defeating giants, and poor, downtrodden women marrying handsome princes. They give us hope.

These basic messages only skim the surface. They have a lot to say about gender, power, roles, marriage, love, and life. It's those messages I will review in this book. My colleague, Helen Argiroff-Flood, and I identified these messages through a content analysis of the Grimms' stories. We learned fairy tales have a great number of hidden messages. Some of the messages were expected, but many were surprising and troublesome. And although the tales seem like a minor form of entertainment, I'll argue they provide us with a fantasy about how life could be for us. They give us hope that one can live happily ever and we can become a king or a queen.

1 | The Importance of Fairy Tales

airy tales are among some of the first stories children learn in many cultures and many people recall being read fairy tales during their early years. These magnificent tales are also prevalent in movie versions that both adults and children enjoy watching. These movies are highly successful, with the 2015 version of Cinderella grossing over $200 million ("Cinderella 2015 total gross," n.d.) and Beauty and the Beast grossing over $500 million domestically in 2017 ("Beauty and the Beast 2017 total gross," n.d.). But there are other movie versions of these classics such as Ella Enchanted and Pretty Woman, which essentially tell the same story of Cinderella. Ella has a wicked stepmother and terrible stepsisters who will stop at nothing to humiliate her. Despite this situation, in the end, she prevails and gets her handsome prince. The movie Pretty Woman doesn't have an evil stepmother, but it's the story of a poor woman who ends up marrying a handsome and wealthy businessman. In works of fiction, such as Pride and Prejudice by Jane Austen, there is a version of the Cinderella story where a downtrodden but good woman ends up marrying a very wealthy man. This story is popular in both the book and movie versions.

The fairy tale has an ancient history. Researchers have determined some stories have prehistoric roots. Beauty and the Beast is believed to be 4,000 years old and Jack and the Beanstalk is about 5,000 years old ("Fairy tale origins," 2016). Cinderella appears in China during the Tang Dynasty (618-

907 CE) in the story of *Yeh Shen* (Mark, 2017). Given its long history, it may have as many as 1,500 versions (Heiner, 2012). The preponderance of fairy tales within the German culture prompted the Brothers Grimm to begin collecting oral fairy tales from friends and family, as well as peasant story tellers, which they published in 1812. The stories are so popular that their collection of fairy tales is the second most read and translated book after the bible (Grimm & Grimm, 2014).

Many might say fairy tales are just entertainment and modern people don't take them seriously. I'd argue that at some level we take them *very* seriously and they impact us in ways we don't even know. One researcher found that children who had been read a fairy tale were more subdued and pensive afterward (Crain, D'Alessio, McIntyre & Smoke, 1983). Perhaps the tale had touched on the children's inner concerns and they were thinking about what they just heard.

Some people believe fairy tales are particularly important to children because they allow them to project any current anger toward the adults in their lives onto truly evil beings, and to ultimately see the downtrodden triumph over evil, which gives children hope. These stories give the child a canvas on which they can work through the major issues of their lives (Kohler, 2014).

Given the prevalence and popularity of fairy tales, it's worth examining them a bit more to see what they have to say. The hidden messages beneath the surface of these stories should bear some scrutiny. It's my contention that fairy tales are instructive about how men and women should behave, how we should deal with obstacles, what behaviors are appropriate, and what behaviors will be rewarded.

According to Reader's Digest (Zeitlin, n.d.), there are nine fairy tales that are most popular: Cinderella, Sleeping Beauty, Beauty and the Beast, Snow White and the Seven Dwarfs, Little Red Riding Hood, Hansel and Gretel, Sleeping Beauty, Jack and the Beanstalk, Puss in Boots, and Rapunzel. There are movie versions of each one of these films and countless children's books with these specific stories.

I'll discuss some of the major aspects of these tales that are noteworthy. However, an analysis of only nine stories is a limited sample on which to make conclusions about fairy tales. Many of these stories come from the

Brothers Grimm collection so I'll discuss that entire collection as the basis for hidden messages in fairy tales—there are 200 stories in the complete book. The only popular fairy tale not contained in this collection is Puss in Boots, which has an animal as its main character. And given that animal behavior may not translate to lessons for humans, I've limited the analysis of stories where humans are the main characters. Let's begin with Cinderella, which is one of the most beloved fairy tales of all time.

2 | Poor Cinderella

inderella is my favorite fairy tale because I like the idea of a poor, hard-working, mistreated girl who eventually finds happiness through marriage to a wealthy prince. Isn't that what most women long for—a man who is financially successful to provide them with a palace and lifestyle? Researchers have found that when it comes to selecting a mate, women tend to look for men with financial resources and men tend to look for women who are beautiful (Buss, 1989). More recently, researchers have found that men tend to value attractiveness more than women, whereas women tend to value intelligence more than men (Milkman, 2018). Did we get this notion women are supposed to be beautiful and men are supposed to be intelligent and successful from the fairy tale? Or does the fairy tale just tap into notions we have about love and romance between men and women?

The Grimms' version of Cinderella describes a young woman who loses her mother and gains a stepmother and two stepsisters when her father remarries. The stepmother and stepsisters mistreat her terribly, but she still manages to go to the King's ball and meet the prince who is looking for a wife. In this version, there is no fairy godmother and no midnight imperative to get home. However, she does lose a shoe and eventually claims her prince by showing she fits the errant footwear. In the more popular version by Charles Perrault (2009), a fairy godmother is introduced into the story and a coach with attendants is created through magic. Interestingly, in this version Cinderella forgives her stepsisters for treating her badly and marries them off to lords. In the Grimms' version, birds peck the stepsisters' eyes out at the wedding and they're permanently blinded.

Perhaps that's why some say the Grimms' version of popular fairy tales is a bit "grim."

Some Issues with Cinderella

As much as I love the Cinderella fantasy, I'm pretty sure she didn't live happily ever after. My first concern is her lack of qualifications for the job she's taking. In both stories, it's clear that Cinderella isn't a royal person and doesn't appear to know how that particular world operates. Both stories suggest she lives in a cottage or middle-class home, making it unlikely she understands the complexities of running a kingdom and being an integral part of it. I'm thinking about the real Princess Diana who was from an aristocratic family in England, but who had no idea what she was getting into (by her own account) when she married Prince Charles. She was often overwhelmed (Taylor, 2017).

The big trade here is that Cinderella is very beautiful and the Prince has status and wealth. The Prince is drawn to her because of her beauty and her amazing gowns. Yes, gowns. Interestingly, in the older versions of both stories, she goes to more than one ball and dazzles him with her fine clothing, which is provided by either a godmother or a magic bird. It's never mentioned in either story that she's clever or interesting. Nor is there any mention of a conversation between the couple—just dancing. The ball has been specifically set up for him to select a wife and it appears that selection will occur primarily based on appearance, given the short time frame. Sadly, beauty fades over time. It would seem Cinderella is bringing less to the party than the prince and therefore her power in that relationship will be low.

My other big issue with Cinderella is that she seems to have some personality disorder that causes her to act like a doormat. She does everything her stepmothers and stepsisters order her to do, even though their behavior is highly abusive. She never protests that she should be treated better by them or refuses to do their bidding. And she never tries to change her current situation or find a new one. At the end of the day, she's so passive that her situation only changes when the prince goes in search of her and rescues her from her abusive home life. Some may think women just weren't ever independent of men in these tales' settings, but the reality is that women throughout the ages have lived on their own due to the loss of husbands or fathers.

Cinderella's Tale Has Clear Messages

The underlying message for women is they should make a bid for a higher status man. That's a problematic message for women who are at the very top of the educational and success pyramid. There are already too few men of equal status, let alone higher status. And higher status men don't tend to marry their equals. They often marry women who are less successful than themselves. This is probably why successful women are less likely to marry and less likely to have children in the United States than their male counterparts (Hewlett, 2002).

When there are huge discrepancies between the status and resources of two people in a marriage, the one who has greater resources will generally have more power (Blood & Wolfe, 1960; Safilios-Rothschild, 1976). Go to the table with less and you'll pay somehow for the privilege to play. This differential power is due to the fact that those with more resources and status have more potential partners available to them and may have less overall emotional investment in the relationship, which gives them more power (Waller & Hill, 1951). When a person knows they can have many other partners, they're less like to stay in an unfulfilling relationship—a behavior we see in several fairy tales where kings decide the queen should be banished.

Cinderella primarily brings beauty to the table (and maybe a good heart). The prince, however, brings much more. We assume he has good looks, title, status, wealth, and a kingdom. He's likely to have many more potential partners interested in him than just Cinderella. When her beauty fades, will he still be so interested in her if that's primarily what she's offering? When we retell this story, are we suggesting women should find men with a higher status, resulting in having less power in that relationship?

The underlying message of Cinderella is that it's worthwhile for women to invest in their appearance and make a play for a man who is out of their league. If they're lovely enough, they can launch into a different social circle. That is certainly the case for some of the wealthy and famous men who have married models. The other message is that passivity is fine and facing abuse without any response will eventually be rewarded. Someone will rescue us from our difficult situation because good always triumphs over evil. Just hang in long enough and magical things will happen.

As a thought experiment, I'd like you to imagine the Cinderella story where we reverse the genders and Cinder is a male character whose father dies and his mother remarries. His new stepfather and stepbrothers treat him terribly but he continues to live with them and do their bidding. A princess is looking for a husband and her father throws a ball so she can choose a spouse. Unfortunately, Cinder's stepfather and stepbrothers tell him he's not allowed to attend. He goes anyway, thanks to his "fairy godfather" who dresses him in a fine tuxedo. He dances with the princess and then leaves, losing one of his shoes in the process. The princess decides to find Cinder and searches throughout the kingdom until she finds a man who fits the shoe. Does that sound silly? Does it work with the genders reversed?

Fairy Tales Live within Us

These messages impact women in a variety of ways. One way is with the idea of having a fairy tale wedding. Put "Cinderella wedding" into Google, and you'll get 51,600,000 results—everything from Cinderella wedding dresses to actual videos of people enacting their version of the fairy tale in their wedding videos. Several observers have noted that in her recent marriage to Prince Henry, Meghan Markle actually wore the same dress Cinderella wore in the 1950's movie (Bonner, 2018).

Cinderella also reinforces the idea that a woman's appearance will determine her status. That's a tough message for those who aren't born beautiful. Obviously, fairy tales are not the only purveyor of that message, but they don't help. This focus on appearance is one reason women around the globe spend billions each year on beauty products and services.

Although wedding gowns and extravagant wedding receptions can make a woman feel she's a princess for a day, I wonder if that should be the goal. Does every woman really want to marry her Prince Charming, someone who has selected her solely for her looks and who has so much power and status he'll be able to call the shots in their marriage? How satisfying will that marriage be for either of them?

I believe Cinderella didn't live happily ever after and the reasons are revealed in the many subtle messages present in the Grimms' fairy tales; particularly in the most beloved ones. In the next chapter, I'll review what fairy tales have to say about marrying up and the reasons it occurs.

3 | Love and Marriage: Who Marries Up and Why?

O ne could argue Cinderella is an isolated tale so we shouldn't focus on it too much. So, what about the other fairy tales? What do they have to say about love and marriage, and particularly about marrying someone of a much higher status like a prince or king? It turns out they have a lot to say. Of the 200 Grimm fairy tales, there are fifty of them where a non-royal person marries a royal one. Thus, a king, prince, or princess marries someone beneath their status in one-quarter of the tales. Perhaps that's why we like them. Among the beloved eight stories, five of them (Cinderella, Sleeping Beauty, Beauty and the Beast, Snow White and the Seven Dwarfs, and Rapunzel) have a female character who marries a prince. The other three stories (Little Red Riding Hood, Jack and the Beanstalk, and Hansel and Gretel) do not.

Both Men and Women Marry Royalty Equally (But for Different Reasons)

Of the fifty stories where people marry up, in twenty-eight of them a non-royal man marries a princess and in twenty-two, a non-royal woman marries a prince or a king (See Table 1: **Marrying Up**, Chapter 10). What differs is the reasons the two genders marry royalty. Male characters marry up as a result of their actions in every single story— through feats of bravery, defeating armies, and killing giants (See Table 2: **Reasons for Male Characters Marrying Up**, Chapter 10). They often rescue princesses and are given the woman's hand in marriage as a reward. Often kings will give impossible tasks to suitors in order to win their daughter. These men prevail and get the girl in the end. Below is an example of a man who marries a princess after saving her.

> *Hans ran and ran without stopping, until he came to the sea shore, and there far, far out on the water, he perceived a little boat in which his faithless comrades were sitting; and in fierce anger he leapt, without thinking what he was doing...He swung his club and gave his wicked comrades the reward they merited and threw them into the water, and then he sailed with the beautiful maiden, who had been in the greatest alarm, and whom he delivered for the second time, home to her father and mother, and married her, and all rejoiced exceedingly. (Strong Hans, Grimm & Grimm, 2014, p. 469)*

In contrast, female characters are often married simply because they're beautiful. Over half of them do so because of their appearance (See Table 3: **Reasons for Female Characters Marrying Up**, Chapter 10). A comparison of males and females who marry up based on their appearance shows that no male character married royalty for this reason (See Table 4: **Female vs. Male Characters Marrying Up Based on Appearance**, Chapter 10). But for female characters, it's a different story. In a couple of stories, the female characters cannot even talk, but their beauty is apparently enough. For example, in the story Our Lady's Child, a king comes upon a mute, naked beautiful woman in the forest.

> *The King of the country was hunting in the forest, and followed a roe, and as it had fled into the thicket which shut in this part of the forest, he got off his horse, tore the bushes asunder, and cut himself a path with his sword. When he had at last forced his way through, he saw a wonderfully beautiful maiden sitting under the tree; and she sat there and was entirely covered with her golden hair down to her feet. He stood still and looked at her full of surprise, then he spoke to her and said "Who art thou? Why art thou sitting here in the wilderness?" But she gave no answer, for she could not open her mouth. The King continued, "Wilt thou go with me to my castle? Then she just nodded her head a little. The King took her in his arms, carried her to his horse, and rode home with her, and when he reached the royal castle he caused her to be dressed in beautiful garments, and gave her all things in abundance. Although she could not speak, she was still so beautiful and charming that he began to love her with all his heart and it was not long before he married her." (Our Lady's Child, Grimm & Grimm, 2014, p. 21)*

If I came upon a naked, mute woman in a forest, I'd wonder what her current issue might be. Mental illness would be at the top of the things I'd be considering. Beauty would not even come into play.

In many stories, just the appearance of a lovely woman is enough to generate a marriage proposal. For example, in Little Brother and Little Sister, a proposal emerges within minutes of meeting.

Then the door opened, and the King walked in, and there stood a maiden more lovely than any he had ever seen. The maiden was frightened when she saw, not her little roe, but a man come in who wore a golden crown upon his head. But the King looked kindly at her, stretched out his hand, and said, "Will you go with me to my palace and be my dear wife?" (Little Brother and Little Sister, Grimm & Grimm, 2014, p. 50-51)

Perhaps this lack of realism is what we love about fairy tales. Few people are likely to propose marriage within minutes of meeting. Clearly love at first sight is alive and well in fairy tale land.

The underlying message, however, is clear. For many women to marry up, they must be beautiful.

Beastly Men

Although beauty is important for female fiancées, appearance isn't as important for male marriage partners. In fact, in several stories, women marry wildly inappropriate partners such as lions, hedgehogs, donkeys, and even an iron stove. In the story Bearskin, a woman is betrothed to a man who has not cut his beard or nails and who has not washed himself in years. Because he wears a bearskin, several characters think he's actually a bear at first. He ends up at an inn and hears a man crying who explains he cannot pay his hotel bill. "Bearskin" pays the bill and the father offers him his daughter as a form of repayment.

> When the old man saw himself set free from all his troubles, he did not know how to be grateful enough. "Come with me," said he to Bearskin; "my daughters are all miracles of beauty, choose one of them for thyself as a wife." (Bearskin, Grimm & Grimm, 2014, p. 326)

The two older daughters reject the unkempt man, but the younger one agrees to fulfill her father's promise and thinks Bearskin is probably a good man. However, she doesn't look forward to the marriage at all and often cries when she considers it. The fact she's honoring a promise made for an inn payment seems extraordinary.

In numerous stories, the father arranges the marriage of his daughter as a reward to another man. In one story, a king betroths his daughter to a donkey who plays a lute. Apparently, this is the king's way of keeping the donkey from leaving his kingdom.

> When the noble beast had stayed a long time at the King's Court, he thought, "What good does all this do me, I shall still have to go home again?" let his head hang sadly, and went to the King and asked for his dismissal. But the King had grown fond of him, and said, "Little ass, what ails thee? Thou look as sour as a jug of vinegar, I will give thee what thou wantest. Dost thou want gold?" "No," said the donkey, and shook his head.

"Dost though want jewels and rich dress?" "No." "Dost thou wish for half my kingdom" "Indeed, no." Then said the King, "if I did but know what would make thee content. Wilt though have my pretty daughter to wife?" "Ah, yes," said the ass, "I should indeed like her," and all at once he became quite merry and full of happiness, for that was exactly what he was wishing for. So a great and splendid wedding was held. (The Donkey, Grimm & Grimm, 2014, p. 433)

One of the other most beloved fairy tales where a woman marries a non-human character is Beauty and the Beast, which has seen great commercial success for Disney with two movies, launched first in 1991 and then in 2017. Between the two movies, they grossed over $700 million domestically in revenue ("Beauty and the Beast 2017 total gross," n.d., "Beauty and the Beast 1991 total gross," n.d.). The movies also launched dolls, costumes, and other merchandise such as watches and jewelry boxes. The original story was published in 1740 by Gabrielle-Suzanne Barbot deVilleneuve, a French novelist. It's seen various revisions over the years and has been republished in shorter and slightly altered versions in the 18th and 19th century (Deutsch, 2017).

The story is about a beautiful woman named "Beauty" who decides to become the prisoner of a beast in order to save her father. She eventually falls in love with the beast who is actually a handsome prince cursed by a witch and transformed into a beast. The only thing that will break his spell is if a young woman falls in love with him in his beastly form. In the 2017 movie version, the beast is a mean and tyrannical person who has been cursed because he refused to help an elderly woman (who is actually a witch who tests him). In the original 1740 version, he's been cursed because he refuses to marry an elderly, ugly fairy who has fallen in love with him. In both versions, the love that Beauty eventually professes for the beast as he lays dying, transforms him into the handsome, young prince he was before the curse. After the transformation, the couple marry and live happily ever after.

Interestingly, although Beauty can see beyond the beast's exterior, it appears that the writer cannot when it comes to descriptions of her character. Beauty is constantly referred to in terms of her outward appearance; clearly one of the major things she's bringing to the arrangement is her attractiveness.

In the movie, the beast is depicted as huge, ugly, and covered in hair. And the beast in the original story is described in the book as hideous and terrifying.

"The Beast made himself heard. A frightful noise, caused by the enormous weight of his body, by the terrible clank of his scales, and an awful roaring,

announced his arrival. Terror took possession of Beauty." (Barbot de
Villeneuve, 2017)

In the original story of Beauty and the Beast, the spell cannot be broken unless the heroine comes to beast's castle voluntarily. And in this story, it's clear Beauty believes she may be killed by the beast.

"Do you come here voluntarily?" inquired the Beast: "and will you consent
to let your father depart without following him?" Beauty replied that she
had no other intention.

"Ah! And what do you think will become of you after his departure?"

"What it may please you," said she; "my life is at your disposal, and I submit
blindly to the fate which you may doom me to." (Barbot de Villeneuve,
2017)

In the 2017 movie, Beauty is first placed into the cell her father occupied, then is offered a permanent room in the castle. She's alone except for the nightly visit she has with the beast. She is told she will no longer see her family. Her existence goes from terrifying to just lonely.

Imprisonment Leads to Love?

Is it normal for a person who is imprisoned to become enamored by their captors? Is this a fairy tale version of the Stockholm Syndrome, where a person who is held hostage eventually forms positive feelings for a captor (Jameson, 2010)? The poster child for this syndrome is Patty Hearst, who was kidnapped and eventually helped her captors rob banks. She was eventually pardoned by President Clinton, who believed she had not acted of her own volition.

Interestingly, the beast from the original story is uninteresting and stupid in his conversation as a result of the curse that's transformed him. And in the 2017 movie, he's downright rude to Beauty and yells at her twice. Why would imprisonment with such a being lead to love? Does this story work when we reverse the genders? If an ugly, stupid woman imprisoned a young, attractive man, would he be likely to fall in love with her over time?

What are we saying to women when we suggest they will love their captors in fairy tales and that they must see beyond the outward appearance and behavior of men, even though others will only see them in terms of their appearance? What are we suggesting to women when we showcase stories where they sacrifice their family ties and live in solitary surroundings? If the outcome is marriage to a handsome prince, is it worth it?

Major Message: Men and women both marry up equally in fairy tales, but women primarily marry royalty because they're beautiful, whereas men marry due to their actions. Women in tales also love and marry animals or highly unappealing partners, including those who imprison them, whereas men do not.

4 | Engagements and Married Life

airy tales also describe what one can expect after the engagement and after the wedding.

Engagements and Poor Memories

Fairy tales often end with the engagement or marriage of the principal characters and the declaration they lived happily ever after. It sounds good, but is it really truthful?

The first major impediments to happiness occur right after the engagement, where some of the characters forget whom they're engaged to. It's one of the key storylines that occur in several Grimms' tales—a prince promises to marry a woman and then completely forgets (possibly due to magic). Often, he will become engaged to another woman and his initial beloved will search for him. In most tales, she will work in a low-level position, such as a scullery maid or cook within his kingdom, just to be near him. She will often go to a ball or public event and wear a gorgeous dress his current fiancée decides she must own.

The deal that's usually struck is the fiancée can have the dress if she lets the woman sleep outside the bridegroom's sleeping chambers. The new fiancée will usually give the man a sleeping potion, so there won't be any conversation through the door. Typically, three dresses are exchanged for three nights. By the third night, he will be wise to the sleeping potion and will remain awake and discover his initial beloved. You might imagine the conversation would be a mixture of anger and regret, but it begins with the old fiancée bemoaning the fact he doesn't remember her, and his sudden realization he promised himself to her.

> *Suddenly his memory returned to him. "Ah," cried he, "how can I have acted so unfaithfully; but the kiss which in the joy of my heart I gave my parents, on the right cheek, that is to blame for it all, that is what stupefied me!" He sprang up, took the King's daughter by the hand, and led her to his parents' bed. "This is my true bride," said he; "if I marry the other, I shall do a great wrong." The parents, when they heard how everything had happened, gave their consent. (The Drummer, Grimm & Grimm, 2014, p. 530)*

So, what's the implicit message here? Perhaps marriage proposals are easy to come by and just as easy to forget? Interestingly, in almost every story, the second bride felt the dresses were adequate compensation for losing a husband. I'm trying to imagine those dresses...

Married Life

Fairy tales are more focused on getting married than on actual marriage. The few descriptions of married life suggest it's a mixed experience. Husbands are described as abusive in several stories, where they threaten to beat their spouses who do foolish things (Wise Folks, Grimm & Grimm, 2014). In one story, a man holds his wife down and presses her head into a pillow until she "falls asleep." (Lean Lisa, Grimm & Grimm, 2014). However, in one story a man beats his wife too often and is punished for it (Sharing Joy and Sorrow, Grimm & Grimm, 2014).

Wives, particularly non-royal ones, are often described as helpmates to their husbands and are often directed to do things such as cook, sell cows, and manage children. They often do as they're told, even when they don't agree. One male character instructs his wife to send each daughter out into the woods to bring him food and each one disappears.

> *On the third morning the wood-cutter said to his wife, "Send our youngest*
> *child out with my dinner to-day, she has always been good and obedient,*
> *and will stay in the right path, and not run about after every wild humble-*
> *bee, as her sisters did." The mother did not want to do it, and said, "Am I to*
> *lose my dearest child as well?" (The Hut in the Forest , Grimm & Grimm,*
> *2014, p. 473)*

She agrees to send the last daughter out, who gets lost just like her sisters.

Although men tend to be in charge, there are several wives who have strong personalities and can make their husbands' lives difficult. One of the more popular tales is The Fisherman and his Wife, where a man catches a fish, who is actually an enchanted prince, and asks to be thrown back. The man does so, but his wife entreats him to return and ask the magic fish to transform her hovel into a small cottage. The fish grants her wish and they own a lovely cottage filled with nice furniture and a pretty yard. Despite this new house, the woman remains unsatisfied and continues to ask for things—she eventually asks and receives castles, kingdoms, and titles until she becomes the Pope. The husband and enchanted fish eventually become disgusted by her greed and the fish eventually puts the couple back in the original hovel.

Marriage looks fairly challenging in the stories where a husband or wife is lazy or stupid. One woman is instructed by her husband to make dinner and she ends up feeding the sausages to the dog, as well as letting a keg of beer pour onto the floor of her basement. And if that's not enough, she eventually forgets her identity (Frederick & Catherine, Grimm & Grimm, 2014). Another wife also suffers from this type of memory loss and runs away from home (Clever Elsie, Grimm & Grimm, 2014). One man is so lazy he cannot bother to take his goat into the field so he marries a woman with a goat so she can take the two goats out together. (Lazy Harry, Grimm & Grimm, 2014).

Grimms' fairy tales also touch on the more serious topics of murder and adultery in marriage. Interestingly, the three stories dealing with adultery only portray women cheating on husbands (The Three Snake Leaves, The Little Peasant, Grimm & Grimm, 2014). There is not one story where the husband is cheating on his wife. And in a few cases, a queen tries to kill her husband (and in two cases succeeds). In Three Snake Leaves, after a king brings his wife back to life, she repays him by trying to murder him.

> A change had, however, taken place in his wife; after she had been restored to life, it seemed as if all love for her husband had gone out of her heart. After some time, when he wanted to make a voyage over the sea, to visit his old father, and they had gone on board a ship, she forgot the great love and fidelity which he had shown her, and which had been the means of rescuing her from death, and conceived a wicked inclination for the skipper. And once when the young King lay there asleep, she called in the skipper and seized the sleeper by the head, and the skipper took him by the feet, and thus they threw him down into the sea. (The Three Snake-Leaves, Grimm & Grimm, 2014, p. 67)

The king dies, but luckily is saved by a servant who brings him back to life.

Second wives seem to be particularly problematic and are very mean to their stepchildren. Cinderella is not an isolated example of this problem. There is not one instance of a stepmother being kind to her stepchildren in any fairy tale. This topic will be explored later when evil is discussed in Chapter 7.

Thus, marriage is a mixed experience for the characters within fairy tales. This sentiment is described well in one story where a woman wishes to marry a man, so she sends the man's daughter with a message about her desire. His reaction and his method of deciding what to do are noteworthy.

The man said, 'What shall I do? Marriage is a joy and also a torment." At length as he could come to no decision, he pulled off his boot, and said, "Take this boot, it has a hole in the sole of it. Go with it up to the loft, hang it on the big nail, and then pour water into it. If it hold the water, then I will again take a wife, but if it run-through, I will not." The girl did as she was ordered, but the water drew the hole together, and the boot became full to the top. She informed her father how it had turned out. Then he himself went up, and when he saw that she was right, he went to the widow and wooed her, and the wedding was celebrated. (The Three Little Men in the Wood, Grimm & Grimm, 2014, p. 56)

Major Message: Engagements don't always lead to marriages, and once they occur, they're not always happy, regardless of whether one marries royalty or not.

5 | Agency in Fairy Tales: Who is Active and Why

I f you want to experience the most passive people in the universe, then meet Snow White, Sleeping Beauty, Cinderella, and a variety of other female characters who let life happen to them. They represent an extreme version of female passivity.

Briar Rose and Sleeping Beauty

The Grimms' version of Sleeping Beauty is called Briar Rose and it's a story about the dangers of not inviting important guests to auspicious occasions. In this story, the king and queen desperately want a child and are eventually granted their desire. When their little daughter is born, the king invites twelve of the thirteen Wise Women to celebrate her birth. Apparently, they only have twelve golden plates so one isn't invited. Each of the wise women bestows a magic gift on the infant until the last one is about to bestow hers. At this point, the uninvited woman joins the festivities and declares that the child will prick her finger and die at the age of fifteen. Because the last woman has not given her magical gift, she changes this curse from death to a deep sleep for 100 years.

All happens as decreed and the young princess pricks her finger with a spindle and falls deeply into sleep for 100 years, along with the rest of the castle. A large and impenetrable hedge of thorns grows around the castle. Apparently, many are aware that there is a beautiful sleeping princess inside, but no one can conquer the thorny hedge. Numerous princes die trying. After 100 years, a prince learns of the famous princess and tries to get into the castle. Although he's well aware that others have tried and died, he remains unafraid. Luckily his timing is right, the hedge parts and he finds the sleeping princess inside and kisses her. She awakes, along with the rest of the castle, and the two are immediately married.

Snow White

This story is about jealousy, specifically the jealousy of a stepmother toward her more beautiful stepdaughter. The wicked stepmother asks her mirror everyday who is the fairest in the kingdom and is happy until Snow White surpasses her in beauty. Snow White is seven-years-old when the mirror reveals she's the prettiest in the land. The queen can't bear to hear that so she has a huntsman take the child into the woods to kill her. Snow White begs for her life, runs away and finds herself at a cottage where seven dwarfs live. The dwarfs invite her to clean and cook for them in exchange for living there. All goes well until the Queen discovers the girl is still alive and she employs various methods to kill her. She starts with lacing her stays too tightly and then moves onto a poisonous comb and then a poisonous apple. The apple eventually does her in and she appears as though she's dead, although she's actually in a deep sleep.

The dwarfs install her in a glass coffin where she appears as radiant as ever and a prince falls in love with her and manages to talk the dwarfs into allowing him to take her back to his kingdom. During the trip, the pallbearers stumble over a tree stump and that jarring motion knocks the piece of poisonous apple out of Snow White's throat. She awakes and the prince immediately proposes marriage to her. The wicked stepmother comes to the wedding and is punished for her misdeeds.

Beautiful (and Sleepy)

In both of these stories, the heroines are unbelievably passive characters who are literally sleeping through much of their stories. The main attribute describing them is their beauty. In the Grimms' fairytale, there is no description of Snow White's character and the only notable thing mentioned is that she does the cooking, washing, sewing, and knitting for them in exchange for her room and board. She is, however, described as the most beautiful female in the kingdom. Sleeping Beauty's character and appearance are the result of the magic bestowed upon her by the Wise Women or fairies.

> *"Meanwhile the gifts of the Wise Women were plenteously fulfilled on the young girl, for she was so beautiful, modest, good-natured, and wise, that everyone who saw her was bound to love her." (Briar Rose, Grimm & Grimm, 2014, p. 169)*

The most active characters in both of these stories are the princes and the evil stepmother. Once again, we're shown passive women who are unfairly treated by other women who are jealous or who have been slighted. Their mistreatment is not due to anything they've done and they're true victims of these stories.

So why is a beautiful, sleeping woman so attractive? Is there an unstated sexual aspect to these stories making them particularly alluring? Or do we associate women with passivity and therefore, a beautiful woman who is sleeping is just representing her gender in a way we can understand? What are we saying to men when we suggest a sleeping woman should be pursued and kissed without their consent? What message are we giving to young girls— that they may awaken from dreams to find themselves claimed by someone they don't know?

An Analysis of Agency

In an effort to understand agency in fairy tales, my firm Beall Research, Inc., coded the Grimms' stories in terms of whether there is an active or a passive male or female character in each story. There are 200 stories and 169 of them have a human as the main protagonist. In these 169 stories, we identified if there is an active male character, an active female character, or both. For example, in Hansel and Gretel, Hansel takes pebbles and puts them along the path so they can find their way home, whereas Gretel pushes the witch into the oven. Therefore, both of these characters are active.

Interestingly, there is no active female or male character in sixteen—or 9%—of the stories. In the remaining 153 tales, there is an active male character in 81% of these stories and an active female character in 28% of them (See Table 5: **Active, Agentic Characters**, Chapter 10). Thus, male characters are generally more active than female ones.

Male characters are most likely to battle giants, take on witches, solve riddles, and generally prevail in situations that seem insurmountable. They are sometimes helped by magical creatures, animals, or humans who bestow special gifts or specific, helpful knowledge. But in the end, they're tenacious, which eventually leads them to succeed in their goals. Sometimes they set out with a desire to tackle the impossible and at other times, they find themselves in situations that are difficult but unavoidable.

Women, in contrast, become active in fairy tales when they're looking for someone—often brothers or a fiancée who jilted them because he forgot they were engaged. As already discussed, this plot is a common one, laden with women doing lowly tasks in order to gain access to him.

However, there are some notable women who are impressive in terms of the actions they take in response to their situations. In The Glass Coffin, a woman rejects the advances of an evil suitor and tries to shoot him. In Fitcher's Bird, a woman outwits a wizard who kidnaps her and alerts her relatives, who then set his house on fire. In The Twelve Huntsmen, a woman is jilted by a king so she and eleven other women (who look like her) join his hunting group and hunt alongside him until he recognizes her and makes good on his promise. And in the Peasant's Daughter, a poor, smart girl marries a king, but angers him. He decides to banish her from his kingdom, telling her she can take the one thing dearest to her. She drugs him and he awakens in her home, where she tells him she took the one thing that mattered most to her: him. He forgives her and they reconcile. And my favorite example of a strong-willed woman occurs in this story.

> *Once on a time when he was riding forth from his castle with his huntsmen,*
> *three girls were watching their cows upon the mountain, and when they*

saw the King with all his followers, the eldest girl pointed to him, and called to the two other girls, "If I do not get that one, I will have none." Then the second girl answered from the other side of the hill, and pointed to the one who was on the King's right hand, "Hilloa! hilloa! If I do not get him, I will have no one." These, however, were the two ministers. The King heard all this, and when he had come back from the chase, he caused the three girls to be brought to him, and asked them what they had said yesterday on the mountain. This they would not tell him, so the King asked the eldest if she really would take him for her husband? Then she said, 'Yes," and the two ministers married the two sisters, for they were all three fair and beautiful of face, especially the Queen, who had hair like flax. (The Three Little Birds, Grimm & Grimm, 2014, p. 310)

Thus, although men are generally the most agentic characters, there are numerous women who are also active. These ladies are not well represented in the most beloved fairy tales, except for Hansel and Gretel.

Major Message: The majority of active characters in fairy tales are male. Females tend to be less agentic, and in the beloved ones like Snow White and Sleeping Beauty, they're actually asleep. There are a few exceptions, but these female characters are not well known or popular.

6 | Who is Powerful and Who Suffers?

ho are the powerful characters in fairy tales? Power is the capacity or ability to direct or influence the behavior of others and/or the course of events. For example, the beast in the story, Beauty and the Beast, has power, but the witch who cursed him also has a great deal of power. Both characters have a huge impact on several people and the situation resulting from the power they wield.

There is probably no greater example of differential power than in the story Hansel and Gretel who find themselves alone in a forest; hungry and looking for shelter. They encounter an old woman who invites them into her cottage, but they soon learn she has a specific agenda, which is grisly to say the least.

The old woman had only pretended to be so kind; she was in reality a wicked witch, who lay in wait for children, and had only built the little house of bread in order to entice them there. When a child fell into her power, she killed it, cooked and ate it, and that was feast day with her. Witches have red eyes, and cannot see far, but they have a keen scent like the beasts, and are aware when human beings draw near. When Hansel and Grethel came into her neighborhood, she laughed maliciously, and said mockingly, "I have them, they shall not escape me again!" Early in the morning before the children were awake, she was already up, and when she saw both of them sleeping and looking so pretty, with their plump red cheeks, she muttered to herself, "That will be a dainty mouthful!" Then she seized Hansel with her shrivelled hand, carried him into a little stable, and shut him in with a grated door. He might scream as he liked, that was of no use. Then she went to Grethel, shook her till she awoke, and cried, "Get up, lazy thing, fetch some water, and cook something good for thy brother, he is in the stable outside, and is to be made fat. When he is fat, I will eat him." Grethel began to weep bitterly, but it was all in vain, she was forced to do what the wicked witch ordered her. (Hansel and Grethel, Grimm & Grimm, 2014, p. 65)

One cannot imagine less powerful characters than children lost in the woods and a more powerful person than an adult with supernatural powers and the means to shelter and feed them.

A Power Analysis

My firm also analyzed who had the most power in each of the Grimms' fairy tales. In 141 of the stories, there was a human who had an impact on others. The individual who had the greatest impact was identified as the person with the most power. For example, in Hansel and Gretel, the little girl ultimately has the most power because she has the greatest impact on other characters when she kills the witch by pushing her into the oven. In eight of the stories, the most powerful individual was not human, but a wolf, Death, St. Peter, The Lord, or the Devil. These characters are non-human males so they were not included in the analysis.

We discovered the most powerful human being was a man 80% of the time (See Table 6: **Most Powerful Character in Each Story**, Chapter 10). It could be a king who made his daughter marry a donkey (The Donkey, Grimm & Grimm, 2014) or a man who learns the power of a magic set of things and uses them against a thief (The Wishing Table, the Gold-Ass, and the Cudgel in the Sack, Grimm & Grimm, 2014).

Women are the most powerful characters only 20% of the time and they're often evil stepmothers who cause problems for their stepchildren. They're also sisters searching for brothers who have been cast under evil spells or women who trying to find bridegrooms who have jilted them. The remaining women who have power tend to be evil witches. However, generally power in fairy tale land is held by men.

Among royalty, male characters again have the most power (See Table 7: **Royalty and Power**, Chapter 10). kings are the most powerful 55% of the time, princes 30% of the time, and princesses are most powerful about 12% of the time. Queens, sadly, are only powerful 3% of the time. Thus, power among royalty resides with kings and princes.

Who Suffers?

One consistent occurrence in fairy tales is suffering. Most tales have at least some level of suffering perpetrated by one character toward others. We coded who causes and receives the most suffering within each story. We defined suffering as any type of physical or emotional pain one character causes another. We coded whether a male or female caused suffering and whether they caused this suffering to a female or male character. Examples of suffering include being mistreated by a stepmother, being kidnapped and/or imprisoned, being eaten, marrying against one's will, being hurt physically, etc. There are many examples. In one tale, a father and daughter find a golden mortar on land that was given to them by the king. And when the father brings it to the king, he suffers as a result.

> He...took the mortar and carried it to the King, said that he had found it in the cleared land, and asked if he would accept it as a present. The King took the mortar, and asked if he had found nothing besides that? "No," answered the countryman. Then the King said he must now bring him the pestle. The peasant said they had not found that, but he might just as well have spoken to the wind; he was put in prison, and was to stay there until he produced the pestle. The servants had daily to carry him bread and water, which is what people get in prison..." (The Peasant's Wise Daughter, Grimm & Grimm, 2014, p. 305)

Suffering can occur for a variety of reason and isn't limited to common folks. Royalty also suffer, sometimes at the hands of their family members. Maid Maleen learned this in the story named after her.

> There was once a King who had a son who asked in marriage the daughter of a mighty King; she was called Maid Maleen, and was very beautiful. As her father wished to give her to another, the prince was rejected; but as they both loved each other with all their hearts, they would not give each other

up, and Maid Maleen said to her father, "I can and will take no other for my
husband." Then the King flew into a passion, and ordered a dark tower to be
built, into which no ray of sunlight or moonlight should enter. When it was
finished, he said, "Therein shalt thou be imprisoned for seven years, and
then I will come to see if thy perverse sprit is broken." (Maid Maleen, Grimm
& Grimm, 2014, p. 537)

Through our analysis, we discovered men cause and receive the most suffering (See Table 8: **Suffering**, Chapter 10). Males cause suffering 61% of the time compared to females, who cause suffering 39% of the time. But interestingly, men tend to suffer the most. About two thirds of the time (63%), men are the ones who suffer, whereas women suffer about one-third of the time (37%).

When one reviews suffering by gender, men cause other men to suffer 39% of the time and cause women to suffer 22% of the time. Women cause men to suffer 24% of the time and they cause suffering for other women only 15% of the time.

The most common type of female-caused suffering is from stepmothers and witches—sometimes from a stepmother who is also a witch. Children suffer most terribly.

Little brother took his little sister by the hand and said, "Since our mother
died we have had no happiness; our step-mother beats us every day, and if
we come near her she kicks us away with her foot. Our meals are the hard
crusts of bread that are left over; and the little dog under the table is better
off, for she often throws it a nice bit. May Heaven pity us. If our mother only
knew! Come, we will go forth together into the wide world. (Little Brother
and Little Sister, Grimm & Grimm, 2014, p. 48)

These results are fascinating because this pattern doesn't hold for the most popular stories. In these tales, women cause the most suffering to other women. Cinderella, Snow White & the Seven Dwarfs, Sleeping Beauty, and Rapunzel are all stories that showcase women doing terrible things to other women—and most of these perpetrators are stepmothers. The other two beloved stories, Beauty and the Beast and Hansel and Gretel, have witches who cause suffering to both males and females. And the other two popular stories, Jack and the Beanstalk and Little Red Riding Hood, don't have a human character who is causing any problems. The wolf is the major antagonist in Little Red Riding Hood.

Who is Confined and Who is Bewitched?

One type of suffering is being confined against one's will—being kidnapped, imprisoned in a tower or dungeon, or being married to a person whom one doesn't want to marry. In the 169 stories, 60 characters are confined against their will. An example of this occurs in the story Maid Maleen who is imprisoned by her father. Another example occurs in Faithful John, which is a story about a king who falls in love with a portrait of a Princess. He has his servant, John, gather golden wares to impress her and they sail to her palace. John poses as a merchant and he entreats the princess to come to his ship to see his wares.

> *"Faithful John was quite delighted, and led her to the ship, and when the King saw her, he perceived that her beauty was even greater than the picture had represented it to be, and thought no other than that his heart would burst in twain. Then she got into the ship, and the King led her within. Faithful John, however, remained behind with the pilot, and ordered the ship to be pushed off, saying 'Set all sail, till it fly like a bird in the air.' Within, however, the King showed her the golden vessels, every one of them, also the wide beasts and strange animals. Many hours went by whilst she was seeing everything, and in her delight she did not observe that the ship was sailing away. After she had looked at the last, she thanked the merchant and wanted to go home, but when she came to the side of the ship, she saw that it was on the deep sea far from land, and hurrying onwards with all sail set. 'Ah, cried she in alarm, I am betrayed! I am carried away and have fallen into the power of a merchant—I would die rather!'" (Faithful John, Grimm & Grimm, 2014, p. 34)*

This story describes a kidnapping, which is clearly confinement against one's will. When we analyzed the number of male and female characters who are imprisoned, confined or married against their will, we found that female characters are more likely to experience this situation than males (See **Table 9: Gender of Character Confined in Story**, Chapter 10).

Amazingly, after the princess in the Faithful John story bemoans being kidnapped, the king explains that he is royal and that it's only out of love for her that caused him to carry her away. Apparently, this answer is sufficiently comforting to the princess and she agrees to become his wife. I'm not sure about you, but I tend to prefer more traditional forms of courtship.

We also analyzed who is bewitched in stories and gets changed into an animal, statue or other inanimate object such as a stove. The most common transformation seems to occur for princes who are changed into frogs, ravens, swans, horses, and other creatures. Witches and wizards are generally behind these spells and they often require some type of feat in order to release the person who has been bewitched. As you may recall in the story Iron Stove, a prince must find someone who will scrape a hole in the exterior of the stove in order to release him. In many stories it's unclear why the person was bewitched. Apparently just wishing that someone is changed can cause that to occur. For example, in the Seven Ravens, a father gets impatient with his seven sons and angrily wishes that they were ravens. As soon has he utters those words, the boys become ravens and fly away. In the story, The Six Swans, a queen who is a witch changes her stepsons in order to get them out of her life.

> *"The children, who saw from a distance that some one was approaching, thought that their dear father was coming to them, and full of joy, ran to meet him. Then she threw one of the little shirts over each of them, and no sooner had the shirts touched their bodies than they were changed into swans, and flew away over the forest. The Queen went home quite delighted, and thought she had got rid of her step-children. (The Six Swans, Grimm & Grimm, 2014, p.166)*

We analyzed whether males or females are more likely to be bewitched. Across the stories, there are 52 characters who are bewitched—21 of them are female and 31 are male. Thus, 60% of those bewitched are men and 40% are women. We conducted a chi-square analysis to determine if this is a statistically significant difference and it's not (See **Table 10: Gender of Bewitched Character**, Chapter 10).

Major Message: Men tend to be the most powerful characters in fairy tales. Among royalty, kings and princes are the most powerful, whereas queens are the least powerful. Male characters tend to cause the most suffering—to other men. But in the eight most popular fairy tales, women have a high degree of power and they primarily cause suffering to other women. Characters who are confined against their will are usually females. But when it comes to being bewitched, male and female characters are equally likely to have a spell cast upon them.

7 | Good Overcomes Evil— But When and For Whom?

Good Overcomes Evil

If you like the idea of a good person prevailing against an evil one, then fairy tales are made for you. And who doesn't like that story? Snow White is one of the best examples of a tale where good characters eventually get what they deserve. Snow White is purely good and her stepmother is completely evil and bent on destroying a defenseless little girl. And why does she want to do this? Simply because Snow White is more beautiful. The stepmother has a strong reaction to this information, which as you know, is conveyed by a magic mirror.

> Then the Queen was shocked, and turned yellow and green with envy. From that hour, whenever she looked at Snow-white, her heart heaved in her breast, she hated the girl so much. And envy and pride grew higher and higher in her heart like a weed, so that she had no peace day or night. She called a huntsman, and said "Take the child away into the forest; I will no longer have her in my sight. Kill her, and bring me back her heart as a token." (Little Snow-White, Grimm & Grimm, 2014, p.178)

One cannot imagine a more hateful person than this queen. The huntsman doesn't kill Snow White and she ends up going to a little cottage of seven dwarfs. But the magic mirror reveals Snow White is still alive and the queen has renewed energy to kill little Snow White.

Interestingly, the dwarfs seem more aware of the potential for this danger to occur than Snow White. They warn her not to let anyone into the cottage, but she's easily fooled and lets the queen into her home when the woman dresses up as a peddler selling wares. Apparently Snow White isn't very intelligent, given that she manages to fall for the same ruse three times.

The balance of power is clear: The queen uses witchcraft to create her disguises and the implements for killing. She also possesses an omniscient talking mirror. Her royal position and skills have made her extremely powerful, especially against a young, rather trusting and somewhat unintelligent girl. But Snow White is eventually saved by a prince who unintentionally manages to dislodge the poisonous apple from her throat.

When the queen learns Snow White is alive and about to marry the prince, she goes to the wedding, where justice is delivered swiftly.

> At first she would not go to the wedding at all, but she had no peace, and must go to see the young Queen. And when she went in she knew Snow White; and she stood still with rage and fear, and could not stir. But iron slippers had already been put upon the fire, and they were brought in with tongs, and set before her. Then she was forced to put on the red-hot shoes, and dance until she dropped down dead. (*Little Snow-white*, Grimm & Grimm, 2014, p. 184)

This story does a great job of showing good overcomes evil—and it's incredibly clear who is good, who is suffering, and who is eventually rewarded and punished.

Who Vanquishes Evil?

As already discussed, suffering is a common part of fairy tales, but who is typically the character who overcomes evil and makes everything right in the end? We identified that in 106 stories there is a clear demonstration of a good person who overcomes an evil one. In the other stories, there was not a clear indication of good overriding evil or the evil characters prevailing in the end. However, stories where evil wins are generally rare.

We conducted an analysis in which we determined which character vanquished evil in each story. For example, a king who condemns a witch to death for her evil deeds would be the person who vanquished evil in the story. Interestingly, the most powerful person sometimes is not the person who eventually sets things straight. For example, witches were sometimes the most powerful people in stories, but they were not the ones who conquered evil.

We found that in 81% of these 106 stories, the person who vanquished evil is a male character, whereas only 19% of the time it's a female (See Table 11: **Vanquishing Evil**, Chapter 10). And in one third of all stories that person who conquers evil is royalty—a king, queen, princess, or prince. However, 81% of these royal characters are men. Thus, men vanquish evil, particularly royal men.

An example of this type of event occurs in the story The White Bride and the Black One. In this fairy tale, a king is fooled into marrying an evil, ugly woman who is the stepsister to a lovely woman he intended to marry. An evil stepmother, who is also a witch, engineers this situation and turns the fiancée into a duck. Apparently, the duck eventually reveals her identity to a kitchen boy. The king cuts the duck's neck and she transforms into the beautiful maiden whom he initially wished to marry.

> *The King was full of joy, and as she stood there quite wet, he caused splendid apparel to be brought and had her clothed in it. Then she told how she had been betrayed by cunning and falsehood, and at last thrown down into the water, and her first request was that her brother should be brought forth from the pit of snakes, and when the King had fulfilled this request, he went*

into the chamber where the old witch was, and asked, What does she
deserve who does this and that?-and related what had happened. Then was
she so blinded that she was aware of nothing and said, "She deserves to be
stripped naked, and put into a barrel with nails, and that a horse should be
harnessed to the barrel, and the horse sent all over the world." All of which
was done to her, and to her black daughter. But the King married the white
and beautiful bride, and rewarded her faithful brother, and made him a rich
and distinguished man. (The White Bride and the Black One, Grimm &
Grimm, 2014, p. 419)

Good, Powerful Men and Bad, Evil Women

If we examine who has power and who is good and evil, an interesting pattern emerges. Powerful men are usually good, whereas powerful women are almost equally split between good and evil (See Table 12: **Goodness, Evil and Gender**, Chapter 10). We conducted an analysis where we classified powerful characters as good or evil. Among powerful male characters, 71% of them are good and 29% are evil (See Table 13: **Male Characters, Goodness and Power**, Chapter 10). However, among powerful female characters, 46% are good and 54% are evil (See Table 14: **Female Characters, Goodness and Power**, Chapter 10). Thus, 1 out of every 2 powerful women is evil, but the majority of powerful men in fairy tale land are benevolent. So, if you come across a man with power, you can probably bet he is good, but with a powerful female character, you're just as likely to find a good apple as a bad one.

So, what's the message fairy tales are saying about powerful women? If they're equally likely to be good or evil, powerful women must be handled very carefully. They can certainly create a lot of suffering and one can't always determine if they're good or evil. Thus, powerful women are risky. Perhaps it's best to assume they're evil unless told otherwise, given the preponderance of them. And isn't that how we sometimes think of powerful women?

This finding reminds me of a Saturday Night Live skit in which the comedian Amy Poehler portrayed Hillary Clinton throwing a Halloween party. She is dressed in a white wedding dress. As she approaches her guests, each one remarks on her great witch costume. When she explains that she's dressed as a bride, they immediately see their faux pas. "Oh, I see it now. It's all in how you wear it, I guess," says one guest at the party (The Clinton's Halloween Party—SNL, 2013).

In fairy tales, powerful female characters range from the obvious witches and stepmothers who are identified as evil from the beginning, to old women with magical powers who often help less powerful characters. One example occurs in the story The Devil with the Three Golden Hairs. A king tries to separate a young husband from his daughter by insisting he fetch three golden hairs from the head of the devil in order to retain his marriage. The man goes to hell, where the devil's grandmother turns him into an ant and pulls out three of the devil's hairs for him. Not only does she give him the golden hairs, she finds out the answers to three major questions he has, which eventually helps him and several other characters in the story (The Devil with Three Golden Hairs, Grimm & Grimm, 2014).

Interestingly, powerful women are generally influential as a result of witchcraft, whereas powerful men are influential because of their position—often because they're royalty. Thus, it appears men have legitimate power, whereas women do not. As already discussed, being royalty tends to beget power only for men, not women (See Table 7: **Royalty and Power**, Chapter 10). Being a queen doesn't necessarily lead one to have power by virtue of one's position. In actuality, witches/stepmothers seem to have the most power.

Royal Men Vanquish Witches

So, what does this all mean? It means in cases where an evil woman is vanquished, it's likely through a good and powerful man, often a royal. The storyline is very clear: an evil witch/stepmother does terrible things and a good king or prince ultimately delivers justice. And the power structure is clear—he has power through a position he holds and she holds power through some type of black arts.

An example of this situation occurs in one story where a queen has just given birth to a little boy and is suffocated by an evil witch and her daughter. The ugly daughter is substituted in the queen's place until the king realizes what's happened. His true queen appears in a ghostly form and nurses her child.

> Then the King could not restrain himself; he sprang towards her, and said, "You can be none other than my dear wife." She answered, "Yes, I am your dear wife," and at the same moment she received life again, and by God's grace became fresh, rosy, and full of health.

> Then she told the King the evil deed which the wicked witch and her daughter had been guilty of towards her. The King ordered both to be led before the judge, and judgement was delivered against them. (Little Brother & Little Sister, Grimm & Grimm, 2014, p. 52)

Witches are featured in the Grimms' fairy tales much more than wizards, who are the male version of this character, and they seem to hold a particularly contemptible position. These women are generally described as ugly and old. Some descriptions liken them to animals.

> "But the wicked step-mother was a witch, and had seen how the two children had gone away, and had crept after them privily, as witches do creep..." (Little Brother and Little Sister, Grimm & Grimm, 2014, p. 48)

> "Witches have red eyes, and cannot see far, but they have a keen scent like the beasts, and are aware when human beings draw near." (Hansel and Grethel, Grimm & Grimm, 2014, p. 65)

Other descriptions suggest that they are human women with special powers.

> "There was once an old castle in the midst of a large and thick forest, and in it an old woman who was a witch dwelt all alone. In the day-time she changed herself into a cat or a screech owl, but in the evening she took her proper shape again as a human being." (Jorinda and Joringel, Grimm & Grimm, 2014, p. 239)

Regardless of the depiction, witches are generally despised. One common thing they do is transform people into animals or inanimate objects like statues. Witches also have the ability to change themselves into various disguises; including animals and attractive women. They sometimes look kind and sweet. Thus, the message is reiterated that powerful women have tremendous powers and are not always obviously evil in appearance. Their true appearance is ugly, but given their ability to transform themselves, one must be on guard. Witches often extract promises or fool their victims into making deals that are extremely disadvantageous.

> "When evening drew near he stopped and looked around him, and then he saw that he had lost his way. He sought a way out, but could find none. Then he perceived an aged woman with a head which nodded perpetually, who came towards him, but she was a witch. "Good woman," said he to her, "Can you not show me the way through forest?" "Oh yes, Lord King," she answered, "that I certainly can, but on one condition, and if you do not fulfil that, you will never get out of the forest, and will die of hunger in it."

> "What kind of condition is it?" asked the King.

> "I have a daughter," said the old woman, "who is as beautiful as any one in the world, and well deserves to be your consort, and if you will make her your Queen, I will show you the way out of the forest." In the anguish of his heart the King consented... (The Six Swans, Grimm & Grimm, 2014, p. 165)

The male version of this character is a wizard and there are few of them in fairy tales. One example occurs in the story Fitcher's Bird (Grimm & Grimm, 2014), where a wizard takes the form of a poor beggar man who captures pretty girls and takes them to his magnificent home and tests them. The women who fail the test are killed. It's gruesome.

Major Message: Powerful men are usually good, whereas powerful women are almost equally split between good and evil. Powerful men tend to be royalty, whereas powerful women are not—they tend to be witches and stepmothers. Royal men are generally the ones who tend to vanquish evil in fairy tales. Thus, good and powerful kings and princes tend to conquer evil, powerful witches/stepmothers (who are not generally royal).

8 | Common Characters and What They Reveal

The most common characters in Grimms' fairy tales are royalty (king, queen, prince, princess), as well as non-royal men such as huntsmen, tailors, woodcutters, and women who range from the older married women to young unmarried ladies. These characters reveal a great deal about what life is like for royalty, as well as for regular people.

Emotions Reveal A Great Deal

Want to know what it's like to be a prince, princess, king, or queen? Our analysis of the emotions each of these characters experience and express reveals a great deal about their inner emotional lives and how they experience different events. These emotions also tell us how they experience major events and the quality of their life during the story.

My firm coded the four major emotions: happiness, sadness, anger, and fear for all the major types of characters (See Table 15: **Characters and Emotions**, Chapter 10). We selected these emotions because they're among the six basic ones identified by psychologists (Ekman, 2007). Psychologists have identified these as the universal emotions because they're identified accurately across cultures. The other two universal emotions are contempt and surprise. We did not code contempt because it's never clearly described in the stories. We also didn't code surprise because it's a momentary expression and doesn't reveal as much about major events and ongoing issues for characters.

Kings

The top of the food chain are clearly kings. As discussed in the previous chapter, they're often very powerful by virtue of their position. However, they're not infallible and they sometimes make errors. A common mistake kings make is being tricked into marrying a non-desirable woman or not recognizing another woman has been substituted for one's wife. An example of this occurs in the story The Three Little Men in the Wood (Grimm & Grimm, 2014), where a stepmother substitutes her ugly daughter for a queen. Eventually he figures it out, but not for a while.

Although kings are occasionally tricked, they tend to be good guys at heart and often do the right thing. One area where they tend to be notable is in marrying women who are suffering. In several stories, a beautiful woman who is being victimized by an evil stepmother is saved by a king who marries her.

> Then the stepmother was still more enraged, and thought of nothing but how to do every possible injury to the man's daughter, whose beauty, however, grew daily greater. At length, she took a cauldron, set it on the fire, and boiled yarn in it. When it was boiled, she flung it on the poor girl's shoulder, and gave her an axe in order that she might go on the frozen river, cut a hole in the ice, and rinse the yarn. She was obedient, went thither and cut a hole in the ice; and while she was in the midst of her cutting, a splendid carriage came driving up, in which sat the King. The carriage stopped, and the King asked, "My child, who are thou, and what art thou doing here?" "I am a poor girl, and I am rinsing yarn." Then the King felt compassion, and when he saw that she was so very beautiful, he said to her, "Wilt thou go away with me?" "Ah, yes, with all my heart," she answered, for she was glad to get away from the mother and sister.

So she got into the carriage and drove away with the King, and when they arrived at his palace, the wedding was celebrated with great pomp..." (The Three Little Men in the Wood, Grimm & Grimm, 2014, p. 58)

Kings usually are the ones who correct injustices—generally at the end of the story. In The Three Little Men in the Wood, the king asks the stepmother what punishment is appropriate for a what she's done and she pronounces the person should be put into a barrel full of nails and then rolled down hill into water. And that's how he punishes her and her daughter.

Not surprisingly, kings are one of the happiest characters and over one-third (41%) of their expressions are happy ones. The emotion they express next in frequency is anger (28%), which some researchers believe is an emotion that occurs when one's goals are blocked by someone (Harmon-Jones & Harmon-Jones, 2016). Anger is highly related to status; people believe those who express anger are more likely to be higher in status (Tiedens, 2001; Tiedens et al, 2000). Thus, anger is related to power and status, so it's not surprising when one of the most powerful, high-status characters expresses anger over one quarter of the time. The expression next in frequency for kings is sadness (25%), followed by fear (7%). Thus, these are powerful, happy characters who are prone to some anger and sadness, but are generally not fearful. In fairy tale land, it's good to be king.

Queens

In contrast, being a queen doesn't appear to be as good of an experience. As already discussed, queens are not powerful and they are often under siege by other women who wish to remove and replace them. A common plot line in numerous stories is the queen is killed or transformed and another woman takes her place. For example, in The Three Little Men in the Wood, a wicked stepmother (who had abused her stepdaughter before she became queen), pays a visit to the queen and throws her into the stream that flows by the castle. Her ugly daughter then takes her place.

Mother-in-laws also try to have queens removed, and in several stories are successful. Queens also have the unfortunate luck of having their children taken from them and are sometimes blamed for their murder. This plot is also common.

> *The King, however, had a wicked mother who was dissatisfied with this marriage and spoke ill of the young Queen...After a year had passed, when the queen brought her first child into the world, the old woman took it away from her, and smeared her mouth with blood as she slept. Then she went to the King and accused the Queen of being a man-eater." (The Six Swans, Grimm & Grimm, 2014, p. 167)*

Sadly, the person who generally pronounces the queen's sentence is her husband. Thus, queens are at the mercy of kings potentially banishing them to fortresses or determining they must be executed.

> *"When they had lived happily together for a few years, the King's mother, who was a wicked woman, began to slander the young Queen, and said to the King, "This is a common beggar girl whom thou hast brought back with thee. Who knows what impious trick she practises secretly! Even if she be dumb, and not able to speak, she still might laugh for once; but those who do not laugh have bad consciences." At first the King would not believe it, but*

the old woman urged this so long, and accused her of so many evil things,
that at last the King let himself be persuaded and sentenced her to death."
(The Twelve Brothers, Grimm & Grimm, 2014, p. 46)

Given the horrendous things that happen to queens and their lack of power, it's no surprise the most common emotion they express is sadness (41%), followed by happiness (34%), which is often due to being saved in the nick of time or being reunited with lost family members. Queens also express fear (14%) and a little anger (10%). Thus, in fairy tale land, being a queen is a dangerous position to have because others are plotting against you and you're at the mercy of kings.

Princes

Princes are among the happiest and most active characters. These individuals tend to save women, often princesses, and they're rewarded by marrying the damsel who was once in distress. Cinderella, Snow White, and Sleeping Beauty all have this story line. However, being a prince can be dangerous.

> *"But round about the castle there began to grow a hedge of thorns, which*
> *every year became higher, and at last grew close up round the castle and all*
> *over it, so that there was nothing of it to be seen, not even the flag upon the*
> *roof. But the story of the beautiful sleeping "Briar-rose," for so the princess*
> *was named, went about the country, so that from time to time kings' sons*
> *came and tried to get through the thorny hedge into the castle.*
> *But they found it impossible, for the thorns held fast together, as if they had*
> *hands, and the youths were caught in them, could not get loose again, and*
> *died a miserable death." (Briar Rose, Grimm & Grimm, 2014, p. 170)*

Princes often exhibit a highly level of daring and they have incredible adventures. Their specific feats of bravery vary. One example occurs in the story The Golden Bird. A prince is asked to find a golden bird, a golden horse, and the princess who lives in a golden castle. He experiences tremendous difficulties to win his prizes and is even thrown into prison. When he finally prevails, his brothers throw him down a well and steal the bird, horse, and princess. Eventually he is rescued and reunited with his animals and his princess. He marries her and is pronounced king.

Princes are very sought-after marriage partners due to their potential to be kings. At times, princes forget whom they've pledged themselves to, but in some cases their parents are the ones who interfere with an engagement.

> *"There was once a King's son who was betrothed to a maiden whom he*
> *loved very much. And when he was sitting beside her and very happy, news*

came that his father lay sick unto death, and desired to see him once again before his end. Then he said to his beloved, "I must now go and leave thee, I give thee a ring as a remembrance of me. When I am King, I will return and fetch thee." So he rode away, and when he reached his father, the latter was dangerously ill, and near his death. He said to him, "Dear son, I wished to see thee once again before my end, promise me to marry as I wish," and he named a certain King's daughter who was to be his wife. The son was in such trouble that he did not think what he was doing, and said, "Yes, dear father, your will shall be done," and thereupon the King shut his eyes, and died." (The Twelve Huntsmen, Grimm & Grimm, 2014, p. 236)

Another downside of being a prince is they're sometimes transformed into animals. Princes are turned into fish (The Fisherman and His Wife, Grimm & Grimm, 2014), lions (The Singing, Springing Lark, Grimm & Grimm, 2014), and a black dog (The Three Little Birds, Grimm & Grimm, 2014). In one case, the prince is turned into a stove (The Iron Stove, Grimm & Grimm, 2014). Luckily, they're almost always restored to their human form—usually by a princess.

Princes express the most happiness of all characters—mostly because they live happily ever after through marriage and often becoming king. Approximately 56% of their expressions are happy, 28% are sad, 8% are angry, and the remaining 8% are fearful. Thus, although they're the most active and adventurous characters, they're not particularly fearful or angry. Mostly they're happy, and occasionally sad. Thus, it's good to be a prince because you're a desired marital partner. The lovely maiden you rescue will likely become your wife unless your parents interfere or you forget.

Princesses

Princesses are fairy inactive and show more fear than any other royal character. It's probably because they tend to be in terrible situations—they're often captured and locked away, desperate to be rescued. Common situations include being captured by a dragon (and in one case being scheduled for its breakfast).

> *"And when the huntsman had taken care of his animals, he asked the innkeeper why the town was thus hung with black crape? Said the host, "Because our King's only daughter is to die to-morrow." The huntsman inquired if she was "sick unto death?" "No," answered the host, "she is vigorous and healthy, nevertheless she must die!" "How is that?" asked the huntsman. "There is a high hill without the town, whereon dwells a dragon who every year must have a pure virgin, or he lays the whole country waste, and now all the maidens have already been given to him, and there is no longer anyone left but the King's daughter, yet there is no mercy for her; she must be given up to him, and that is to be done to-morrow." (The Two Brothers, Grimm & Grimm, 2014, p. 210)*

Luckily, a huntsman saves her, marries her, and becomes king.

Princesses are often punished and taught a lesson when they're too haughty or who have made promises they don't intend to keep. The lesson almost always comes from a father or other man. In one case, a young princess loses her golden ball in a water and a frog rescues it in exchange for the promise he will be her play thing and eat and sleep with her. She agrees to this deal, but then promptly leaves the frog once he returns her golden ball. The frog is undeterred and presents himself at the castle. The princess explains her dilemma and the king promptly insists she stand by her word.

"That which thou hast promised must thou perform. Go and let him in." She
went and opened the door, and the frog hopped in and followed her, step by
step to her chair. There he sat and cried, "Lift me up beside thee." She
delayed, until at last the King commanded her to do it...The King's daughter
began to cry because she was afraid of the cold frog...But the King grew
angry and said, "He who helped thee when thou wert in trouble ought not
afterwards to be despised by thee." (The Frog-King or Iron Henry, Grimm &
Grimm, 2014, p. 17)

The most impressive version of a royal teaching a princess a lesson occurs in the story King Thrushbeard (Grimm & Grimm, 2014). A beautiful, haughty princess won't accept any suitor—none are good enough for her. She even makes fun of them. She says one suitor has a chin like a thrush's beak and from that point on they call him "King Thrushbeard." Her father becomes so exasperated with her that he claims the next beggar who comes to the castle will be her husband. A fiddler comes to the castle and the king fulfills his promise: she is resigned to a life of poverty. At several points, she wishes she had married the king with the crooked chin, but she's resigned to her fate. When she goes to her family's castle to see her brother's wedding, she sees King Thrushbeard, who reveals he is the fiddler she married and he had disguised himself during their marriage. She promptly asks for his forgiveness (and we assume they live happily ever after).

But regular men also teach princesses lessons when they believe they're superior to others, particularly brave suitors who wish to marry them. For example, in The White Snake (Grimm & Grimm, 2014), a servant competes for the hand of a beautiful princess by pulling a golden ring from the bottom of the sea (with the help of some fish friends). Although he does the impossible, the princess is unmoved and insists he pick up every seed that has fallen to the ground from 10 millet sacks. And when he accomplishes that mission, she requests he get the apple from the tree of life. When he does so, she falls in love with him.

Princesses are often happy, sad, and fearful. Almost half (44%) of their emotions are happy due to living happily ever after, one quarter are sad (26%), and almost that many are fear (22%). Given the scary situations they're in and the lessons they endure, the sadness and fearful expressions are to be expected. The least expressed emotion is anger (7%), which is surprising given that they're often put in awful situations. So, if you're a princess, don't be too haughty. And if you're in trouble, hold on because your man is likely on his way.

Stepmothers

Stepmothers are generally described as "wicked" and "old." Every stepmother in the Grimms' fairy tales is evil and does horrific things to her stepchildren. They verbally abuse them, deprive them of food, make them do impossible tasks, turn them into animals, and attempt to kill them or actually do so. Not one stepmother is ever described as being kind to her stepchildren.

Stepmothers are mostly angry (71% of expressions) and occasionally fearful (14%) and happy (14%), but never sad (0%). As described earlier, anger is an emotion associated with status and power, but it's also an indication of frustration with people and situations they're trying to control. And because that's largely what they express, they're clearly not getting their way. Evil characters like stepmothers are almost always vanquished. Apparently, if you're a stepmother, you're definitely evil and will actively try to hurt your stepchildren, but you'll eventually be frustrated and won't get your way.

Witches

Witches are also described as "wicked," "ugly," and "old." They can also be stepmothers, which is the worst combination. Witches are among the most powerful characters because they cause a lot of suffering for people. However, they're almost always punished for their misdeeds. The most common emotions this type of character expresses is anger (58%), fear (29%), a small amount of happiness (14%), and some sadness (7%). Thus, this is a powerful character who doesn't get to have a lot of fun. The message for witches is you will have a huge influence, but you will eventually get defeated and you won't have a lot of fun along the way.

Old and Young Non-Royal Women

Non-royal women fall into two types: an older, powerful woman who helps other characters and a younger woman who is not powerful. Older, powerful women sometimes give less powerful characters extremely useful information. For example, in the story The Shoes That Were Danced to Pieces (Grimm & Grimm, 2014), a king wants to know where his twelve daughters go at night because their shoes are always worn out in the morning. Several princes try to solve the mystery and fail. A soldier decides to try his hand at the mystery and he encounters an old woman who tells him not to drink the wine he's served at night by the princesses. She also gives him an invisible cloak. He solves the mystery and ends up marrying one of the princesses as a result.

These old, powerful women also provide access to important people like the devil or giants. They sometimes help characters obtain impossible things that have been requested like three golden hairs from the head of the devil. A king tells a man he can't marry his daughter unless he fetches the three golden hairs from the devil. The suitor goes to hell to find the devil and encounters his grandmother, who transforms him into an ant and hides him in the folds of her dress. She pulls out three of his hairs while he sleeps and also asks the devil to answer several questions the man poses to her. She is the sole reason he can marry the princess (The Devil with the Three Golden Hairs, Grimm & Grimm, 2014). And like many of these old, powerful women, she doesn't express any emotions at all; she just helps him.

The other type of woman is a younger woman who isn't powerful at all. The single, beautiful women are often passive, tend to suffer, and are rewarded like Cinderella. The married ones are usually helpmates to their husbands and can sometimes be stupid or problematic. In general, these powerless non-royal women express a variety of emotions, with the most common ones being sadness (31%), happiness (26%), fear (25%), and anger (18%). The message is clear for powerless female characters: If you're unmarried, beautiful, and good, you may marry a prince or a king.

Non-Royal Men

Non-royal men tend to be tailors, huntsmen, soldiers, millers, and servants. These male characters are typically unmarried and can be smart, fearless, or foolish, but they sometimes accomplish impossible tasks, overcome evil people, and end up marrying princesses or gaining major positions within a kingdom as a result. Non-royal men express all types of emotions, especially happiness and fear. As you may recall, fear was not expressed much by princes or kings, so it's interesting to see the regular man experiences and expresses it, whereas the royal man does not. Most common expressions among these non-royal men are happiness (33%), fear (26%), anger (21%), and sadness (19%). The message here is that a non-royal man can gain a princess and/or a great position, but it will be an emotional ride.

Other Male Characters

Other male characters include the devil, death, the Lord, St. Peter, dwarfs, and wizards. These characters are relatively rare. The devil is obviously evil and he strikes deals with humans, but he can be outsmarted. His predominant emotion is anger. Wizards are often evil, yet can be defeated. Death can't be reasoned with or defeated and it doesn't express any emotions. The Lord and St. Peter make things right when situations are out of control and they don't express any emotions. Dwarfs can be evil or good (e.g., Snow White). Evil dwarfs' express anger and can be defeated. The message is evil male characters can be outsmarted, even the devil, but powerful male characters cannot.

Overview of Male Characters

Character	Degree of Power	Good or Evil	Emotional Expressions	Outcomes
King	Powerful	Good	Mostly happiness	Maintains power and distributes punishment
Prince	Powerful	Good	Mostly happiness	Usually marries beautiful maiden or princess
Non-royal man	Some power, usually the result of intelligence or bravery	Mostly good	Happiness followed by fear	Obtains princess or position as a result of actions; evil characters always punished
Devil	Powerful	Evil	Anger	Devil can be outsmarted
Wizard	Powerful	Generally evil	Anger	Usually brutally punished for being evil

Summary: Most male characters are powerful. And most powerful, good male characters are happy.

Overview of Female Characters

Character	Degree of Power	Good or Evil	Emotional Expressions	Outcomes
Stepmother	Powerful	Evil	Mostly anger	Usually brutally punished
Witch	Powerful	Evil	Mostly anger	Usually brutally punished
Queen	Somewhat powerful	Good	Mostly sadness and some happiness	Often under attack and usually saved in the end
Old woman	Somewhat powerful	Good	None	Helpful to other people
Princess	Generally, not powerful	Good	Happiness, sadness, and fear	Usually saved by a prince, but sometimes taught lesson
Non-royal women	Not powerful	Good	Sadness, fear, and happiness	If unmarried, beautiful and good, may marry royalty

Summary: Most powerful female characters tend to be evil and are punished.

9 | Other Messages in Fairy Tales

airy tales are a rich source for other messages that are worth discussing.

Follow Instructions or Else!

One of the messages in many fairy tales is following the rules is paramount. It doesn't matter how crazy the instruction is, you must follow it or you're going to have some major problems. This lesson is aptly conveyed in Little Red Riding Hood, or Little Red Cap, as it's called in the Grimms' stories. Little Red Riding Hood's mother warns her to stay on the path and not to tarry on the way to her grandmother's house. As a result of not following this advice, she and her grandmother both get eaten by the wolf. Luckily, a huntsman saves both of them when he cuts the wolf open and sets them free. Apparently, the wolf ate them whole.

Not following instructions can result in death, as it did for one little girl who was warned not to visit an old woman by the name of Frau Trude. Her parents insist the old woman is a witch and if she goes to visit, they will disown her. Undeterred, she goes to visit and the witch turns the little girl into a block of wood and throws her into the fire (Frau Trude, Grimm & Grimm, 2014).

Other instructions are less clear and almost bizarre, but characters who follow them are rewarded. In Faithful John (Grimm & Grimm, 2014), a loyal servant to the king dies and becomes a stone who can talk. He explains to the king if he kills his two children and sprinkles their blood on him, he will live again. The king convinces his wife that they must do this terrible deed, which restores the servant to life. Luckily, the children are also restored.

Be Nice to Animals

In many fairy tales, being nice to animals has tremendous rewards and being unkind to them is severely punished. Kindness to animals is sometimes rewarded by the animals themselves. In The White Snake (Grimm & Grimm, 2014), a servant frees three fishes who are caught in the reeds, he avoids trampling some ants by taking his horse around them, and he feeds some fledgling ravens. Each creature says the same thing to him: "We will remember you—one good turn deserves another!" When he needs to find a golden ring at the bottom of the ocean, the fish get it for him. When he has to sort seeds, the ants do the task, and when he needs to find the apple from the tree of life, the ravens obtain it for him. His ability to procure these objects lands him the king's daughter.

In other cases, the animals instruct characters on how to obtain what they desire. For example, in the story The Golden Bird (Grimm & Grimm, 2014), a fox tells the youngest prince what he has to do in order to gain a golden horse, a golden bird, and a golden princess. His first two brothers don't listen to him and one remarks: "How can such a silly beast give wise advice?" The prince who takes this advice eventually obtains what he desires.

Attractive People are Never Old

Beauty and age are always intertwined in the world of fairy tales. Those who are beautiful are never referred to as being old. Old women and old men are never described as attractive, and the most physically attractive characters are generally unmarried, which is an indication of age. Ageism is alive and well in fairy tales.

Magic is a Part of Everyday Life & People Aren't as They Appear

In the world of fairy tales, becoming bewitched and being transformed into a stone, a statue, or an animal are everyday occurrences. And a person's appearance can be distorted to be ugly or old. In one story, a man goes to rescue a beautiful princess in a castle and is surprised by what he finds.

> *"He entered and went through all the rooms, until in the last he found the King's daughter. But how shocked he was when he saw her. She had an ashen-gray face full of wrinkles, blear eyes, and red hair. "Are you the King's daughter, whose beauty the whole world praises?" cried he. "Ah," she answered, "this is not my form; human eyes can only see me in this state of ugliness, but that thou mayst know what I am like, look in the mirror it does not let itself misled it will show thee my image as it is in truth." She gave him the mirror in his hand, and he saw therein the likeness of the most beautiful maiden on earth, and saw, too how the tears were rolling down her cheeks with grief. (The Crystal Ball, Grimm & Grimm, 2014, p. 536)*

Magic is so common in fairy tales it's described as something to be expected. In one story, a couple walks too close to a witch's castle and the woman is transformed into a nightingale when the man looks away from her. The witch also works her magic on him and he's unable to move or speak until the witch leaves (Jorinda & Joringel, Grimm & Grimm, 2014). All of this is stated as if it's completely normal and expected.

Expect Miracles

Because magic is so commonplace, one can always expect miracles in fairy tales. Dead people are brought back to life, those who have been incapacitated are restored, and blind people regain their eyesight. In one particularly impressive example, a tailor is blinded by another man and finds himself underneath gallows where the two dead men are hanging. Surprisingly, the men are able to talk to one another in death.

> *"Then one of the men who had been hanged began to speak, and said "Brother, art thou awake?" "Yes, I am awake," answered the second. "Then I will tell thee something," said the first; "the dew which this night has fallen down over us from the gallows, gives every one who washes himself with it his eyes again. If blind people did but know this, how many would regain their sight who do not believe that to be possible?*
>
> *When the tailor heard that, he took his pocket-handkerchief pressed it on the grass, and when it was moist with dew, washed the socket of his eyes with it. Immediately was fulfilled what the man on the gallows had said, and a couple of healthy new eyes filled the sockets." (The Two Travelers, Grimm & Grimm, 2014, p. 339)*

Characters Like the Devil and the Lord Walk among Us

Another noteworthy aspect of fairy tales is how characters like the Devil and the Lord live and interact with human beings. The devil and "Death" each make agreements with various male characters in a few fairy tales. Often the agreements involve a level of service for a certain number of years or doing specific things, such as not bathing for a set amount of time.

> *"A disbanded soldier had nothing to live on, and did not know how to get on. So he went out into the forest and when he had walked for a short time, he met a little man who was, however, the Devil. The little man said to him, "What ails you, you seem so very sorrowful?" Then the soldier said, "I am hungry, but have no money." The Devil said, "If you will hire yourself to me,*

and be my serving-man, you shall have enough for all your life? You shall
serve me for seven years, and after that you shall again be free. But one
thing I must tell you, and that is, you must not wash, comb or trim yourself,
or cut your hair or nails, or wipe the water from your eyes." (The Devil's
Sooty Brother, Grimm & Grimm, 2014, p. 322)

Interestingly, the devil can be fooled. In one story, a man ends of making a fool of the devil and obtaining a large treasure by agreeing to give the devil the things that grow above the soil. But that season, he grows turnips. The devil then wants the things that grow beneath the soil the following season, and the peasant then grows wheat (The Peasant and the Devil, Grimm & Grimm, 2014).

The Lord, in contrast, doesn't create agreements, but occasionally appears as a character who needs assistance. In one story, the narrator explains there was a time when God resided on earth and he has very human needs.

"In olden times, when the Lord himself still used to walk about on this earth
among men, it once happened that he was tired and overtaken by the
darkness before he could reach an inn." (The Poor man and the Rich Man,
Grimm & Grimm, 2014, p. 276)

The Lord ends up rewarding those who treat him well.

10 | Methodology and Data from Grimms' Fairy Tales

W e employed a content analyst for this work, which is a common method of analyzing literary texts. Every fairy tale with humans as the major characters was read at least twice before coding them. The author was the primary person who coded the 169 stories and another individual coded 129 of the stories in order to ascertain whether there were any biases on the part of either person. The two people used specific definitions for coding and analyzed each story individually, without consulting one another. The correlation between the coders was .93, which means that the ratings were the same for 93% of all codes. For the specific codes, there was 88% coding agreement for active vs. inactive characters, 96% agreement for coding of evil and power, 100% for marrying up, 97% for suffering and 84% across all of the emotions that were coded.

Below are the definitions that were used.

Definitions

Marrying up: A non-royal person marrying or becoming engaged to a prince, princess, king or queen.

Agentic/Active characters: Characters who express an interest in a specific goal and then take specific actions toward achieving the objective even when there are obstacles that impede their progress.

Most agentic/active character: The character who engages in the most actions designed to achieve desired goals.

Power: Having a positive or negative impact on another character through specific actions that are intended to have an impact on them.

Most powerful character: The character who has the greatest positive or negative impact on other characters.

Suffering: A negative physical or emotional experience not desired by the character.

Confinement: Being imprisoned or unable to leave a situation (e.g., being locked in a tower) that is not desired. This definition includes being married against one's will.

Bewitched: Having a spell cast upon a particular character that altered the person's appearance or changed the character into an animal, statue, etc.

Evil Characters: Characters who consistently act in ways designed to cause suffering or the destruction of one or more characters

Defeating Evil: Punishment of evil characters and/or the restoration of wronged characters to their rightful positions.

Emotion Coding

Emotions of characters were coded based on the description of the character having one of four emotional experiences: happiness, sadness, anger, and fear. We determined these emotions provided us with the most information about the inner life of the characters and the quality of their lives in the story.

Happiness: Character was described as being happy or experienced a major event that was positive in nature, such as being reunited with a loved one, released from a spell, or saved from an emotionally/physically difficult situation. Characters who were described as "living happily ever after" were also coded as being happy.

Sadness: Character was described as sad or displayed tears.

Anger: Character was described as angry or yelled at another character.

Fear: Character was described as afraid or fearful.

Data

As Table 1 shows, males and females marry up at about the same rate. We calculated a chi-squared statistic, which determines whether the data is similar to what would be expected by chance. As you can see below, the data is not statistically different than what would be expected by chance— so there is not a statistical difference in terms of the number of male versus female characters who marry up.

Table 1: *Marrying Up*

Gender of person marrying royalty	Number of characters	Percentage
Male	28	56%
Female	22	44%
Total	50	100%

Chi-squared equals 0.729, $p=0.3961$ (not statistically significant)

Table 2 shows males are likely to marry up completely because of their actions.

Table 2: **Reasons for Male Characters Marrying Up**

Reasons male characters marry princesses/queens	Number of characters	Percentage
Appearance	0	0%
Actions	28	100%
Total	28	100%

Chi-squared equals 28.00, p< .0001 (statistically significant)

Table 3 shows females are more likely to marry up because of their appearance.

Table 3: **Reasons for Female Characters Marrying Up**

Reasons female characters marry princes/kings	Number of characters	Percentage
Appearance	13	59%
Actions	9	41%
Total	22	100%

Chi-squared equals 0.727, p=0.393 (not statistically significant)

Table 4 shows that no male married up based on their appearance. However 13 female characters married royalty simply because they were attractive.

Table 4: **Gender and Marrying Because of Appearance**

Gender of character marrying up because of appearance	Number of characters	Percentage
Females	13	100%
Males	0	0%
Total	13	100%

Chi-squared equals 11.14, p=0.008 (statistically significant)

Table 5 shows male characters are more likely to be active than female characters.

Table 5: **Active, Agentic Characters**

Gender of active characters	Number of characters	Percentage
Male	124	74%
Female	43	26%
Total	167	100%

Chi-squared equals 38.32, p<.0001 (statistically significant)

Table 6 demonstrates male characters are much more likely to be powerful than female ones.

Table 6: **Most Powerful Character in Each Story**

Gender of most powerful character	Number of characters	Percentage
Male	112	79%
Female	20	21%
Total	132	100%

Chi-squared equals 64.12, p<.0001 (statistically significant)

In Table 7, kings and princes are the royalty most likely to have power. Kings are over half of royal power characters.

Table 7: **Royalty and Power**

Royalty characters with Power	Number of characters	Percentage
King	18	55%
Queen	1	3%
Prince	10	30%
Princess	4	12%
Total	33	100%

Chi-squared equals 17.62, p=.0005 (statistically significant)

Table 8 shows how men cause the most suffering and men suffer more than women. Not surprisingly, men also cause the most suffering toward other men.

Table 8: **Suffering**

Gender	Number of characters	Percentage
Males causing suffering of males	95	39%
Males causing suffering of females	52	22%
Females causing suffering of males	57	24%
Females causing suffering of females	37	15%
Total	241	100%
Chi-squared equals 28.94, p<.0001 (statistically significant)		
Overall males causing suffering	147	61%
Overall females causing suffering	94	39%
Chi-squared equals 11.22, p=.0008 (statistically significant)		
Overall men suffering	152	63%
Overall female suffering	89	37%
Chi-squared equals 15.95, p<.0001 (statistically significant)		

In Table 9, it's clear that female characters are confined against their will more often than males

Table 9: *Gender of Character Confined in Story*

Gender Confined	Number of characters	Percentage
Female characters	39	65%
Male characters	21	35%
Chi-squared equals 5.4, p = .02 (statistically significant)		

In Table 10, although men are bewitched in stories slightly more than women, this result is not statistically significant.

Table 10: *Gender of Bewitched Character*

Gender Bewitched	Number of characters	Percentage
Female characters	21	40%
Male characters	31	60%
Chi-squared equals 1.9, p = .165 (not statistically significant)		

In Table 11, it's clear men vanquish evil the most. Royalty vanquish evil about one-third of the time.

Table 11: *Vanquishing Evil*

Gender	Number of characters	Percentage
Men vanquishing evil	87	81%
Women vanquishing evil	20	19%
Chi-squared equals 40.71, p<.0001 (statistically significant)		
Royal person vanquishes evil	33	31%

In Table 12, it's clear good powerful men are more common than any other type of character.

Table 12: **Goodness, Evil and Gender**

Gender	Number of characters	Percentage
Good, powerful men	141	49%
Evil, powerful men	58	20%
Good, powerful women	42	14%
Evil, powerful women	49	17%
Total	290	100%

Chi-squared equals 86.57, p<.0001 (statistically significant)

In Table 13, good powerful men are more common than evil, powerful men.

Table 13: **Male Characters, Goodness and Power**

Gender	Number of characters	Percentage of Male Characters
Good, powerful men	141	71%
Evil, powerful men	58	29%

Chi-squared equals 33.79, p<.0001 (not statistically significant)

In contrast, there is almost an equivalent number of good and evil powerful women.

Table 14: **Female Characters, Goodness and Power**

Gender	Number of characters	Percentage of Female Characters
Good powerful women	42	46%
Evil, powerful women	49	54%

Chi-squared equals .40, p=.70 (not statistically significant)

Table 15 shows the most common emotions by character. The number in bold is the emotion experienced the most by each character. As shown below, happiness is experienced the most by kings, princes, princesses, and non-royal men and women. Queens experience sadness the most, and stepmothers and witches experience anger more than any other emotions.

*Table 15: **Characters and Emotions***

Character	Anger	Sadness	Fear	Happiness	Total
King	28% (19)	24% (17)	7% (5)	**41%** (28)	100% (69)
Queen	10% (3)	**41%** (12)	14% (4)	34% (10)	100% (29)
Prince	8% (3)	28% (10)	8% (3)	**56%** (20)	100% (36)
Princess	7% (5)	26% (18)	22% (15)	**44%** (30)	100% (68)
Stepmother	**71%** (10)	0% (0)	14% (2)	14% (2)	100% (14)
Witch	**59%** (10)	7% (1)	29% (4)	14% (2)	100% (17)
Non-royal men	21% (38)	19% (34)	26% (47)	**33%** (59)	100% (178)
Other non-royal women	18% (20)	31% (35)	25% (28)	**26%** (29)	100% (112)

King Chi-squared equals 14.26, p=.002 (statistically significant)
Queen Chi-squared equals 7.64, p=.05 (almost statistically significant)
Prince Chi-squared equals 21.65, p<.0001 (statistically significant)
Princess Chi-squared equals 18.7, p=.0003 (statistically significant)
Stepmother Chi-squared equals 21.66, p<.0001 (statistically significant)
Witch Chi-squared equals 8.25, p=.04 (statistically significant)
Non-royal men Chi-squared equals 8.06, p=.04 (statistically significant)
Non-royal women Chi-squared equals 4.07, p=.25 (not statistically significant)

11 | Final Thoughts

After reading these findings, you may wonder why does this matter? Why should we care if fairy tales are sexist and women are passive and often saved? What does it matter if men are always the powerful, active characters? How does it matter if powerful men are good and powerful women are equally likely to be good as evil? It's just a story.

Fairy tales are more than entertaining stories; they're a huge part of our culture. The commercial success of these fairy tales leads one to realize these stories are not just fanciful stories. By telling and retelling these narratives we convey more than the plot lines—we convey the hidden messages, as well. The little girl who hears the tale of Cinderella, Snow White, and Sleeping Beauty learns women are victimized, passive, and that attractive women are lucky to be saved by a handsome prince. Is this a good message to give them?

Anita Baker's song Fairy Tales speaks to the reality of how women grow up with expectations based on fairy tales and how they're deeply disappointed later in life. She sings about how she remembered her mother telling her fairy tales before she went to bed and imagined her future prince arriving, saving her, and making her happy. Instead she experiences a relationship filled with screaming, crying, betrayal and eventually abandonment. Her song claims that her mother's bedtime stories led her to expect a life that was unrealistic.

Researchers have investigated the impact of princess culture on children as young as preschoolers and have found staggering results. In a study of 198 preschoolers, researchers found that 96% of girls and 87% of boys had been exposed to Disney Princess media with 50% of girls and 29% of boys viewing such media at least once a month, and 61% of girls playing with Disney Princess toys at least once a week. (Coyne et al, 2016). The investigators determined that girls who engaged the most with Disney Princess media strongly identified with princess culture and tended to have more stereotypical ideas about gender. They also behaved in more gender-stereotypical ways (as observed by teachers and parents). Interestingly, this effect was observed one year later, which suggests that princess culture has a long-lasting impact (Coyne et al, 2016). The concern is that girls who strongly identify with this culture will be more passive, less likely to think of themselves as being good at math and science, and more concerned with their appearance to the detriment of other aspects of self. In fact, in one study, adult women who saw themselves as "princesses" were more likely to give up on a challenging task, less likely to want to work, and more focused on superficial things (Dinella, cited in Coyne et al, 2016)

One concern with princess culture is the tremendous focus on appearance, which psychologists are concerned is detrimental to girls. The American Psychological Association has discovered that a significant focus on appearance leads girls to be more prone to depression, eating disorders, and low self-esteem (APA, 2007). Self-objectification, which is the degree to which one looks at oneself as an object, (whom others view only in terms of appearance), is linked to impaired performance on mathematical tasks and logical reasoning (APA, 2007)

More Recent Disney Princesses

It appears that Disney is trying to create some more up-to-date fairy tales where women are more active and less likely to be saved by a prince. Certainly, the movie Frozen is a step in the right direction with a focus on sisterly love and reuniting family members, not finding a handsome prince. In fact, one of the main characters, Anna learns how handsome princes can be nefarious and one should closely inspect suitors for ulterior motives. In her case, the handsome prince is only looking for a seat on the throne and doesn't care for her at all. She ends up being more interested in an ice salesman with a good heart, but there is no mention of love or marriage between them. The happily ever after occurs when she and her sister forgive one another and are reunited.

The movie Brave is also a good example of a more progressive movie where the focus is on the relationship between the young woman and her mother, rather than on winning the hand of a royal man. Her parents wish to arrange a marriage with one of the clansmen (or princes) in her area and she resists. She ends up visiting a witch and accidentally turning her mother into a bear. The rest of the movie is about how she and her mother repair their relationship and realize the importance of their bond. The movie doesn't end with a happily ever after due to marriage to anyone. The happiness is due to the mother-daughter reunification.

Maleficent is another Disney movie that's a version of Sleeping Beauty with a twist. In this movie, the evil witch has a love affair with Stefan, a man who eventually becomes king. Stefan cuts off her wings and eventually marries someone else. When he and his wife have a little girl, Aurora, they invite the kingdom to celebrate her christening. The rest of the story is similar to Sleeping Beauty, with Maleficent showing up uninvited for the ceremony where she casts a spell that Aurora will fall into a lengthy sleep on her sixteenth birthday. All goes as planned, except Maleficent becomes fond of the young girl and eventually is the one who awakens her with a kiss. It's not a handsome prince who loves her, but a woman who comes to view her like a daughter. The idea that women saving other women outside of a love relationship is not typical of a fairy tale.

These movies are popular and profitable. Frozen had revenue of 400 Million ("Frozen 2013 total gross," n.d.), Brave grossed 237 million ("Brave 2012 total gross, n.d.), and Maleficent grossed 241 million ("Maleficent 2014 total gross," n.d.) in the United States. Although each of these revenue numbers is less than the Beauty and the Beast, (which grossed around 500 million ("Beauty & the Beast 2017 total gross," n.d., Beauty & the Beast, 1991 total gross," n.d.)), they're more than the revenue for Cinderella, which grossed around 200 million ("Cinderella 2015 total gross," n.d.). Clearly, these non-traditional fairy tales are very appealing. Researchers claim there is some evidence that Disney princes and princesses are becoming somewhat less traditional and more complex in their characters (Whitbourne, 2014).

These new ways of thinking about happily ever after suggest it's not about marriage or finding the prince (or princess), but about the bonds we form across many different relationships. It is one's actions across several relationships providing one's happily ever after. These new stories may lead us to think differently about the world and what we want within it.

Why Cinderella Didn't Live Happily Ever After

I'm afraid that things are unlikely to go well for Cinderella given the hidden messages that were uncovered in our analysis. Because she will be a queen, she'll have little power and be under attack by various women who wish to take her place. If she has a mother-in-law, she may be especially dangerous because she may want her son to be with a different and potentially royal woman. Given how most queens fare in the stories, she'll most likely be sad and fearful. Her power will be limited because her husband, the king, will be the one who will determine her fate. And if she does gain any power, people may worry she's evil, as many powerful women are believed to be. Lastly, because she's already shown she's passive, she will be greatly at risk to be abused and not stand up for herself.

We all would like to believe Cinderella lived happily ever after, but it's unclear whether she actually understands what she's getting herself into at this point. The desire to be saved and to marry a handsome prince may actually be her undoing. So, we wish her luck. And if you're a person who desires to live a fairy tale, be warned; it looks like there is a large part of the story that isn't communicated.

Anne E. Beall, Ph.D.

Anne E. Beall is CEO and founder of Beall Research, Inc. She specializes in strategic market research and previously worked at the Boston Consulting Group (BCG). Anne conducts both qualitative and quantitative market research around the world. She specializes in conducting large-scale, complex strategic studies for Fortune 500 companies.

She has written the following books: *The Psychology of Gender* (Eagly, Beall & Sternberg, 2005), *Reading the Hidden Communications Around You: A Guide to Reading Body Language in the Workplace*, *Strategic Market Research: A Guide to Conducting Research that Drives Businesses*, *Community Cats: A Journey Into the World of Feral Cats*, and *Heartfelt Connections: How Animals and People Help One Another.*

Beall received her M.S., M.Phil. and Ph.D. degrees in Social Psychology from Yale University. In her spare time, she enjoys running and walking on the Chicago lakefront, as well as sampling the many city restaurants.

References

American Psychological Association (APA) (2007). Report of the APA Task force on the sexualization of girls: Executve summary. Retrieved from https://www.apa.org/pi/women/programs/girls/report

Averill, J. R. (1983). Studies on anger and aggression: Implications for theories of emotion. *American Psychologist*, 38, 1145-1160.

Barbot de Villeneuve, G (2017). The story of beauty and the beast (R. L. Lawrence, Adaptation and J. R. Planche, Trans.,). Blackdown publications (Original work published 1740).

Beall, A. E. (2019). *Reading the Hidden Communications Around You: A Guide to Reading Body Language in the Workplace*. Chicago: Independent publishing

Beall, A. E. (2019). *Strategic Market Research: A Guide to Conducting Research that Drives Businesses*. Chicago: Independent publishing.

Beall, A. E. (2019). *Community Cats: A Journey Into the World of Feral Cats*. Chicago: Independent publishing.

Beall, A. E. (2018). *Heartfelt Connections: How Animals and People Help One Another*. Chicago: Independent publishing.

Beauty and the Beast 2017 domestic total gross sales (n.d.). Box Office Mojo Website. Retrieved from https://www.boxofficemojo.com/movies/?id=beautyandthebeast2017.htm.

Beauty and the Beast 1991 domestic total gross sales (n.d.). Box Office Mojo Website. Retrieved from https://www.boxofficemojo.com/movies/?id=beautyandthebeast.htm.

Blood, R. O., & Wolfe, D. M. (1960). *Husbands and wives: The dynamics of married living.* New York, NY: Free Press.

Bonner, M. (2018, May 19). Wait, Meghan Markle was literally a Disney princess at the royal wedding. Cosmopolitan website. Retrieved from https://www.cosmopolitan.com/entertainment/a20755918/meghan-markle-disney-princess-wedding-dress-cinderella/.

Brave 2012 domestic total gross sales (n.d.). Box Office Mojo Website. Retrieved from https://www.boxofficemojo.com/movies/?id=bearandthebow.htm.

Buss, David M. 1989. Sex Differences in Human Mate Preferences: Evolutionary Hypotheses Tested in 37 Cultures. *Behavioral and Brain Sciences.* 12, 1-14.

Cinderella 2015 domestic total gross sales (n.d.). Box Office Mojo Website. Retrieved from https://www.boxofficemojo.com/movies/?id=cinderella2015.htm

Coyne, S. M., Linder, J. R., Rasmussen, E. E., Nelson, D.A., & Birkbeck, V. (2016) Pretty as a Princess: Longitudinal Effects of Engagement With Disney Princesses on Gender Stereotypes, Body Esteem, and Prosocial Behavior in Children, Child Development, November/December 2016, Volume 87, Number 6, Pages 1909–1925.

Crain, W. C., D'Alessio, E., McIntyre, B., & Smoke, L. (1983). The impact of hearing a fairy tale on children's immediate behavior. *The Journal of Genetic Psychology*, 143, 9-17.

Deutsch, J. (2017, March 15). The storied, international, folk history of Beauty and the Beast. Smithsonian Website. Retrieved from https://www.smithsonianmag.com/smithsonian-institution/storied-international-folk-history-beauty-and-beast-180962502/

Eagly, A. H., Beall, A.E, & Sternberg, R.J. (2005). *The Psychology of Gender* (2nd Edition). New York: The Guilford Press.

Ekman, P. (2007). *Emotions revealed: Recognizing faces and feelings to improve communication and emotional life.* New York: Henry Holt.

Fairy tales' lyrics (n.d.). Google website. Retrieved from https://www.google.com/search?q=fairytale+lyrics+anita+baker&spell=1&sa=X&ved=0ahUKEwiZw_jYssXdAhUs74MKHSwEBCoQBQgqKAA&biw=1272&bih=587&dpr=1.5.

Fairy tale origins thousands of years old, researchers say. (2016, Jan 20). BBC Website. Retrieved from https://www.bbc.com/news/uk-35358487.

Frozen 2013 domestic total gross sales (n.d.). Box Office Mojo Website. Retrieved from https://www.boxofficemojo.com/movies/?id=frozen2013.htm.

Grimm, J. & Grimm W. (2014). *The original folk and fairy tales of Grimm Brothers: The Complete First Edition.* CreateSpace Independent Publishing Platform

Harmon-Jones, E. & Harmon-Jones, C. (2016). Anger. In J. F (Barrett, M. Lewis, & J. M. Haviland-Jones (Eds.), *Handbook of Emotions* (4th Edition) (pp. 774-791). New York: Guilford Press.

Heiner, H. A. (2012). History of Cinderella. SurLaLune Fairytales Website. Retrieved from http://www.surlalunefairytales.com/cinderella/history.html.

Hewlett, S. A. (2002). Executive women and the myth of having it all. Harvard Business Review Website. Retrieved from https://hbr.org/2002/04/executive-women-and-the-myth-of-having-it-all.

Jameson, C. (2010). The "Short Step" from love to hypnosis: A reconsideration of the Stockholm Syndrome. *Journal for Cultural Research*, 14:4, 337-355, Retrieved from https://www.tandfonline.com/doi/full/10.1080/14797581003765309

Kohler, S. (2014). On the importance of fairy tales. Psychology Today Website. Retrieved from https://www.psychologytoday.com/us/blog/dreaming-freud/201406/the-importance-fairy-tales.

Maleficent 2014 domestic total gross sales (n.d.). Box Office Mojo Website. Retrieved from https://www.boxofficemojo.com/movies/?id=maleficient.htm.

Mark, J. J. (2017, March 23). The Egyptian Cinderella story debunked. Ancient History Encyclopedia Website. Retrieved from https://www.ancient.eu/article/1038/the-egyptian-cinderella-story-debunked/

Milkman, K. L. (2018, Feb 12). In experiments, researchers figured out what men and women really want in a mate. Washington Post Website. Retrieved from https://www.washingtonpost.com/news/wonk/wp/2018/02/12/in-experiments-researchers-figured-out-what-men-and-women-really-want-in-a-mate/?noredirect=on&utm_term=.1727ddfac0ba.

Safilios-Rothschild, C. (1976). Macro- and micro- examination of family power and love: An exchange model. *Journal of Marriage and the Family*, 38, 355–362. doi:10.2307/350394

Schwartz, C. R. & Han, H. (2014). The reversal of the gender gap and trends in marital dissolution. *American Sociological Review*, 74 (4) 605-629.

Taylor, E. (2017, Aug 15). Princess Diana's most riveting and revealing quotes in Diana: In her own words. Vogue Website. Retrieved from https://www.vogue.com/article/diana-in-her-own-words-national-geographic-powerful-quotes

The Clinton's Halloween Party—SNL (2013). YouTube Website. Retrieved from https://www.youtube.com/watch?v=Njyg0ZzfhyI.

Tiedens, L. Z (2001). Anger and advancement versus sadness and subjugation: the effect of negative emotion expressions on social status conferral. *Journal of Personality and Social Psychology*, 80 (1) 86–94. https://doi:10.1037/0022-3514.80.1.86. PMID 11195894.

Tiedens, L.Z., Ellsworth, P. &Mesquita, B. (2000). Sentimental stereotypes: Emotional expectations for high-and low-status group members. *Personality and Social Psychology Bulletin*, 26 (5) 560 – 575. Retrieved from https://doi.org/10.1177%2F0146167200267004.

Perrault, C. (2009). The complete fairy tales. Oxford: Oxford University Press.

Waller, W. W., & Hill, R. (1951). *The family: A dynamic interpretation*. New York, NY: Dryden Press.

Whitbourne, S.K. (2014, Nov 29). Why do women want fairy tale weddings? Psychology Today Website. Retrieved from https://www.psychologytoday.com/blog/fulfillment-any-age/201411/why-do-women-want-fairy-tale-weddings.

Zeitlin, A. (n.d.). The most popular fairy tale stories of all time. Readers Digest Website. Retrieved from https://www.rd.com/culture/most-popular-fairy-tale-stories/

Index